DEDICATION

This book is dedicated to my brother, Giò (Joey), who I affectionally call my King of Pain. Honoring his memory and sharing some of his pain through my eyes and experiences so that those suffering with the same struggles can find the hope and peace needed to live each day with optimism, strength and victory.

Diary of a Fat and Mourning Post Pandemic Woman

A Journey of the Ebbs and Flows of Grief and Weight Loss

ANN MARIE THRIVES

Diary of a Fat and Mourning Post Pandemic Woman, A Journey of Faith, Grief and Wellness

Ann Marie Thrives

ISBN: 979-8-9894811-4-9 - Softcover
ISBN: 979-8-9894811-5-6 - ebook

Comfort Print

All Scriptures quoted or referenced are taken from the KJV, NKJV or other authorized and free versions.

Table of Contents

Introduction

Diary of a Fat and Mourning Post Pandemic Woman

A Journey of the Ebb and Flow of Grief and Weight Loss

My Story of Grief, Wellness, Mindset, and Victory, Coming Out of the Dark After the Pandemic

Thank you for purchasing this book. This is a story of my wellness and mindset journey before, during, and after the pandemic. How I handled the grief of the homegoing of my brother Joey, and the other losses surrounding me. I was mourning so many things. The loss of my life as I knew it, my body as I knew it, my business as I knew it, my relationships in life as I knew them.

It's a diary of my attempts to reclaim my body, to rejuvenate, rebuild, and restore what was once broken.

I pray that this gives you hope and peace that you are not alone in your grief or health journey. That God is always for you and with you.

There are resources available to you to help you in this journey and through life, and I am one of them.

Blessings to you my dear sister or brother who reads this!!

CHAPTER 1

The Little Girl In the Mirror

One morning, as I was waiting for an answer to a message online, I kept walking back and forth from my computer to the bathroom mirror. I'd do parts of my skin care and color routine and walk back to check for a reply. During a return to check, a picture popped up that made me gasp. It had such an impact that it brought me back in time! It reminded me of one of my school pictures where I was chunky, awkward, well-rounded, and not in the nice traditional way where you've got it together in your areas of life! It was one of those pictures that had a young me and now me. When you look at the NOW picture next to it, you see the beautiful woman who morphed from that plump little girl, and they seem like two different people. I can see the pain in the little girl's eyes and the joy in the eyes of the woman today.

I walked back to the mirror, and when I looked into it, a picture of that young me popped into my head. I could see that old picture as clear as day. Then I saw the me that was now in the mirror. I was two different people, but the same person. I didn't realize how much that shook me and how I wished I could hug that little girl right now. If she could see forward to today, her life would have been a little easier and more hopeful. She would have seen that this girl had a pretty good life and that those moments of deep pain she was experiencing were temporary, and that one day the pain would be different. At that very moment, I heard "Diary of a Fat and Mourning Post-Pandemic Woman," and I knew deep in my heart I had to share this experience.

I had to share the pains of being in a place of loathing and come out. In a place of grief and come through. Remembering back, without going back, and digging deep to love and heal that plump, confused, berated, and hopeless little girl. They never saw the inside of her, the beautiful heart and mind she had. They judged her from the outside, from the fat around her face and chin, the protrusion of her chest and belly, or whatever their eyes landed on first.

They don't see the pain that brought us to this place; the childhood we experienced that caused us so much turmoil that we had to build a wall to hide ourselves and escape the pain of it. They don't see that it was so bad that we had to turn to food because there was no one else to turn to. All they seemed to see was a poor little slob who had no self-control.

This particular Summer of 2020, I lost and gained the same 5 pounds about 5 times because my body was at a critical point in the "big loss," and it was adjusting to its new setpoint while breaking through old barriers. Every meal that I treated myself to that was slightly off-kilter from my current course caused that gain. It may have just been water weight, but it reflected on the scale, and it was discouraging. So, more workouts and smarter choices to get rid of the aftermath of that one meal. It was daunting to my emotions and brain.

I had to consistently remind myself that this was my life journey, not a destination to reach. A lifestyle, not a goal. An abundant lifestyle is a daily goal with healthy habits attached to it. This is our only life. It's a long-term thing. Abundance isn't a one-time goal you reach, and when you're done, you're done. This is something you will be managing for the rest of your life. You don't pee once and never pee again. You don't poop once and never poop again in life. Yes, I know it's gross, but you have to think of this as something that is part of your daily life, just like anything else.

Getting to our "goal weight" is a journey, not a destination. It is also not a one-and-done deal. Yes, you can get there and maintain it for life. I've seen it done by so many people. I stayed at my goal weight for years, but for me, at times, the smallest of things have upset this particular apple cart. Mainly through physical illnesses and other issues contributed to my not being able to work out and follow my plans.

These life challenges did a few things to me. First, they took away the freedom in my body. I was no longer free to express myself through aerobic dance, a good bike or treadmill workout. It also took away the agility in my mind. The serotonin that is produced when we get to the zone in our minds from working out has great benefits to our brains, and it is vital to our healthy life, body, and mind.

So, here's my journey, diary and all!

CHAPTER 2

Rockin' The Pandemic

In October, before the pandemic hit, my husband and I decided to start taking better care of our bodies. We began looking into meal plans that would help us scale down and stay on track. We also started getting more intentional about our daily exercise.

A week into the new meal plan, I had a business trip. I took some of the specific foods I needed to help keep me on track and worked out at the hotel gym. I decided that after my event was over, I would have a reward meal on the way home. It wasn't too much of a stray from what I was currently doing. I just made it a little more interesting by adding butter and sour cream to my potato, having coffee, and a few bites of a cinnamon roll.

As soon as we were home, I was right back on track with my meal plan and continued to exercise. A couple of weeks later, I had a wedding. I was excited to have the opportunity to do the bride's makeup and attend her ceremony and reception.

I allowed myself to try everything and even went back for seconds on a couple of the foods I really liked. The next day, I went right back to my plan.

That Thanksgiving, I made all of our favorite dishes with a healthy twist. Surprisingly, we liked them better than the traditional versions of them. I made my green bean casserole with fresh ingredients, no canned beans or mushroom soup. Instead, I used frozen beans and fresh mushrooms along with my own soup as a substitute. This new way of eating also included making my own pie crusts, using healthier flour alternatives. I ate what I wanted over the weekend and once our company left, you guessed it; I went right back to it!

This continued throughout the Holiday season and into the next year. What I learned during this time is that when I got right back on track, I didn't feel the regret, bloating, or experience the gain that I used to. When it was a Holiday or special event, I chose to eat what I liked, and then I continued to keep going. It was all about my choices. I chose to put the new eating plan aside just for those days or those meals, then continue with it once those special occasions ended.

Sometimes it felt like it was going to take forever to lose the weight and reach my goal. At one point, I was losing and gaining the same 5 pounds for 3 months before there was a breakthrough. I prepared myself ahead of time so that I would have maximum success. I tried different meal plans so that my palate and scale wouldn't get stagnant. I took a couple of trips and maintained. The habits and systems I had put into place were working beautifully for me.

What did I do?

I started going to bed at the same time each night to keep my circadian rhythm. I woke up at the same time, and eventually, my body was waking up at that time on its own.

I had all of my exercise gear ready and in my workout room. All I had to do was get in there, put on my clothes and headset, which was ready to play my favorite get-going and keep moving tunes, and just start.

I was determined that no matter what happened; I was going to stay on track with my health journey. I sought God and asked for help. I asked for specific things to keep me on track, and the plan kept unfolding with each prayer request.

There was a new me that I was working on. I felt pretty good! My future looked promising. My weight was at a good place, and I was having a great time getting there. It was a joint and personal effort. I was working on myself, and we were working on each other. We shared this thing too. Our eating plan, exercise plan, and weigh-ins, watching each other move forward in this desire to optimize our health.

And then it happened. I received news that my brother had passed away. It was unreal, and trying to deal with the reality and grief was more than I could take on. I began to slip and not get right back to it. I started baking like the frog in the pot. The water temperature was going up, but it did not move me one bit. It happened a little at a time, pound by pound, 5 here, 5 there, and the next thing I knew, almost all of it was back.

Mentally, it was horrible. Because I was appeasing myself with food, I was now dealing with two things: grief and lack of self-control. I couldn't seem to stop myself. I didn't want to stop myself. I guess I just wanted to be numb. I was in a place of deep sadness and numbness, slowly drifting, creating a hole so big that I couldn't get myself out. I wanted to stop before it got worse, but somehow, I couldn't.

I had lost hope. In my mind, I kept replaying the pain of what I went through to get to my goal. I was afraid I couldn't handle that again. I had spent months losing slowly. It was grueling having to watch everything I put in my mouth. Then, I sustained an injury that prevented me from working out, and that just added to the misery.

What was different? What went wrong? Circumstances in life happened, and I chose food to deal with them, which caused the compound effect. When there's no break from madness and cheating, it piles up like dirt in the corner, and this kind can't be swept under the rug. If you don't stay ahead of it, it can quickly go from 5 to 10 to twenty, etc. Something manageable can quickly become out of control. Then, instead of it taking a couple of days to get back on track, it could take months.

The upsets of the past few years have changed life and the world for everyone. Many are experiencing grief in different forms, to the point that sometimes we're not sure if we're mourning, even when we are. We've become masters at stuffing feelings and making everything look good on the outside, while on the inside, we are bleeding. We're not sure who to trust, who to turn to, and how to behave. I've run out of fingers and toes counting things I'm mourning. These years have been rough. There has been a disconnect. At first, I thought I was rocking it, and then the bottom fell out.

How do you get it back? The Word says that He turns our mourning into dancing. In my opinion, there's been a lot of mourning for all of us these past few years. We're all grieving something. It could be people, dreams, or our past selves. It could be something we did that we were proud of, but those glory days have now escaped us. We are mourning the loss of things that have died in our lives. We are mourning treasured ones we've lost, dreams that have been unrealized, crushed by a force no one saw coming.

What are you mourning?
Are you still mourning?
Do you know if you're mourning?
Will you let Him, the God of all peace and comfort, turn your mourning into dancing?

CHAPTER 3

Pandemic Uncertainty

The uncertainty of the past few years created a veil over me, like a netting that was holding me back, keeping me cocooned and immobile. I started feeling an overwhelming fear of moving forward and making purposeful decisions and changes.

For a while, the cocoon protected and helped me grow in my spiritual walk until it didn't. I felt like David in the Psalms, where one moment he expressed his situation, oppression, and depression, and then only moments later he'd cry out to God for help.

I felt that even in the darkest of times, despite the physical and emotional pain I was experiencing, I had to reach deep within myself to dig up the trust that God knew this was coming and that He was going to help me. He would give me the hope and strength I needed to break through and glean from this experience and continue in the hope that can only be found in Him and His Word.

Since the beginning of time, God has wanted an abundant life for us (John 10:10). His desire is for us to be mentally and physically agile, free to go about our lives and fulfill His Kingdom business. I needed to draw and cling to everything I had learned and taught... I needed to use these new situations to find creative ways to continue to improve and win in life. It was time to break free of the cocoon and become the butterfly that God created me to be.

Let's look at self-care during these past few years. I feel it has gone in two directions. Some have increased their cognizance of taking care of themselves and have extensively explored different ways of doing so. Sadly, others have gone in another direction. They have given up essential care for themselves and thus have spiraled downwards spiritually, physically, mentally, physically, and emotionally.

Fortunately, or unfortunately, I have experienced both. I had many days, weeks, and seasons where I was rocking my self-care, and then something happened to throw me off track.

Turns out, my brain and emotions were not prepared for this particular life curveball. Between the pandemic, the deaths and disappointments, I was blindsided and slowly fell back to my familiar eating habits not prioritizing my self-care, especially in that regard. I let go of the reins on my life and began seeking comfort in places that were not good for me.

I stayed up longer than my body could handle. I ate more than necessary. I consistently made unhealthy food choices because those foods were giving me the comfort I thought I desperately needed. I reverted to my prior tendencies to calm myself with things that hindered and eventually hurt me.

When we are at the top of our game, close to the Holy Spirit, gleaning our peace and guidance from Him, we can more easily help others be on top of their game in life and share examples of the miracles that hope in God can create.

I fell from being at the top of my game all the time and was on top for short periods of time. It was like a bulimic getting nutrition and then vomiting it out. I spent time with God, and then I went right back to my craziness. I didn't know how to cope with the grief and the shame of how I was dealing with that grief.

CHAPTER 4

Coming Out Of The Dark

Towards the end of December 2019 and into the beginning of 2020, I had a strong sense in my spirit to go online. I kept hearing those words, go online. I had no idea what that would entail. I obeyed and got myself a website for the purpose of sharing what the Lord put on my heart. Maybe through a blog? With the Holy Spirit as my guide, I knew I was going to rock whatever this new thing was.

This was a huge step of faith for me, as I had been doing the same thing for most of my life, and now just one puzzle piece for what was to come next. Once I made the decision to proceed with what little information I had, "go online," I shared it with a couple of friends who took a step back but encouraged me nonetheless.

One day, I was reading an article, and I saw the potential of what could happen if I continued with this, and suddenly, there was a wonderful blessing for my obedience. Not too long afterwards, it all hit the fan, and everyone was online.

I went into task mode and disciplined myself in all areas. I took care of my body, ate well, and put systems in place to get a handle on what I could control because there seemed to be so many things at that time that were out of our control. I went to bed early to help with my circadian rhythm. I got up and worked out, showered, and got into clean jammies. We all remember those multiple sets, right?

In July of 2020, the Lord gave me the word "Crown" from Psalm 103, a Psalm of David, v.4 in The Passion Translation: "You've rescued me from hell and saved my life. You've crowned me with love and mercy."

This is one of my favorite Psalms because of the way it starts, asking God to bless our souls and for our souls to bless God, and continues with the reminder for us not to forget all the benefits He provides, along with His immense mercy toward us.

I later heard the Lord expand on that Word and say to me that He was going to crown the year. Psalm 65:11 says, "You crown the year with Your goodness, And Your paths drip with abundance." I'm Italian, and the word "Corona" translates "Crown," and when I saw that, I had an "Oh Wow" moment.

At the time, I had no idea what that Word would end up meaning for me. As we know, the world had been in upheaval by the middle of March. My surroundings seemed uncertain. Churches, businesses, and schools had been closing all around us. But deep within me, I was determined and hopeful that God would somehow make that Scripture a reality in my life.

The year culminated with losing track of my precious brother Joey, who lived in Italy. He was nowhere to be found, and his phone kept going to voicemail. I prayed, and the skies opened. Little bits of information started trickling in. Someone said that he had fallen and was rushed to the hospital. Another said that he coded while in transit, so they airlifted him to another hospital that could better help him.

After months of trying to track down which hospital he was in, getting bits and pieces of third-hand information on his condition, we finally learned, in a very displeasing way, that he had passed away. It's funny how the enemy takes the hatred that's within people and allows them to use the delivery of delicate news as a sword to intentionally pierce and wound our hearts.

Because of the strength and peace that had been built up with my consistent time with God throughout the year, I saw it for what it was and did not waver. Like Esther in the Bible, I knew where that ugly thing was coming from, and I took action in my spirit and proceeded with His guidance in the natural.

Despite the bewilderment and grief I was experiencing, the Lord brought people into my life to help me with my specific desires to remedy the situation in the best way possible from an ocean away. What I could not do with my own hands, the Lord did for me, and He answered the desires of my heart for my brother in ways that only He could.

With all that was happening, and the entanglements of the legal and international red tape, the Blood of Jesus over the situation was more powerful than all those ugly weapons forged against me. Although the situation seemed hopeless, the Lord was working on my behalf.

And with this grief, you guessed it, the scripture, Psalm 65:11, came to my mind. "So, God, how will You crown this year for me?" was my question to Him. I was trying to stand on that specific Word to glean hope in a hopeless situation.

Memories started flooding in. I started remembering that my brother had talked about this day since my Dad's diagnosis of Lewy Body Disease and imminent death in 2016. Joey couldn't picture a life without my Dad, even making the statement that he wasn't going to be living too long after him. He was miserable in his own body, and as I reflected, I realized that in one fell swoop, God answered everybody's prayers. Life was now different, again, with the loss of another key person in my life.

Where are you experiencing pain? Where did it originate? Can you go back and identify a time in your life where one instance started it all for you, or was it all one straw piling on top of another until you just broke?

Are the majority of those memories you go back to triggers that reignite trauma and cause you to curl up into a ball, rendering you fearful and immobile, or are they milestones that you can smile at because they eased you into the next phase of life?

CHAPTER 5

Death Comes To My King Of Pain

Where did it start for you, my sweet King of Pain? You were so beautiful and so full of joy in your heart. You could laugh at the weirdest things and take me down that road with you.

From before you were in the womb, trouble came. There was distress, and in that distress, you were formed. Maybe you wrestled inside and felt it. There was a push-pull in your life, even before you came out. That push and pull was one of a relationship going on outside of you that had the same effect, and you felt the repercussions of it. One minute you were one way, and the next minute you were another.

You talked at a later age than most, and you had your own words for objects that no one could understand unless they saw you point to them and identify them with you, and then they could communicate. You looked at us like we were nuts for not understanding you.

You were restless. Never in one place for too long. You could not be held still, even when restrained. You had to be about doing things and getting into stuff. That was just you.

You had to go exploring, finding new things, and looking at stuff all around you. Mischief? Curious? Oftentimes, it took a few minutes, and sometimes all it took was seconds, and you were gone, like a bolt of lightning.

You were wild, and no one could hold you in. You were your own person, and yet, there was a gentleness about you when your true heart came out.

You were a prankster and a teaser. You tortured, sometimes until you got your way. You were relentless in so many ways.

Little did we know what was really going on inside of you. You wanted help but did not take it. Many were there to help you out of the pit that you were in. You took the help at times, and then, when things got good, you somehow found a way to make them bad.

Maybe that push and pull from the beginning gnawed at you your whole life. The two natures fighting against each other inside of you.

You were good because you loved people. But when the love of self came, those thoughts of doubt and fear, you believed them and ran with them. Forsaking others, but not yourself.

You weren't taught to fight them off and to subdue them with the Word. You weren't taught how to fight them. We couldn't understand you, so we couldn't teach you, and then it was too late.

Too much damage had been done. There were too many repercussions, and there was essentially a corner turned, and there was no way back.

You tried so many times to make changes, but they never stuck. You would only get so far, and that leash would just yank you back. So many times, you turned over a new leaf. Everyone said the same of you. When you were good, you were awesome, and when the other part of you showed up, you were like no one that they had ever seen. A terror for people to be fearful of. It's hard to believe that this one sweet person could be these two people.

You left a remnant for us that is in a cage herself, yet free. Unable to speak or communicate in some ways, but she makes herself known. She is like you in so many ways. Innocent, quirky, funny, gentle, loving, and willing to be loved.

An image of you that we can still see and find pieces of you in. Oh, how I wish we could draw her out of there and bring her home! To hear her thoughts and to hear her voice. What does she think inside her head? Can she form thoughts, and is she smarter than what we think? I believe so. I believe she is a loving genius inside.

To hear your voice again would be such a delight. You were either in or out, and time with you was brief. You were absent a lot and times spent together felt few and far between. You were gone for periods of time and then would reappear. Like hide and seek. Much like your inner man, so were you on the outside.

You were there, and then you weren't. You were present, and then you were far off. You were cognizant and then oblivious. But never without a plan. Even if the plan was a failure, you had one. You were always scheming inside your head. I could always see the wheels turning. Always looking for the next high, in search of the rush. Why is that?

You were brutal in finding it. You tore down everything you could from anyone, no matter what standing they had in your life. When that call came, you used anyone and anything to answer it. You allowed it to become more powerful than you, so that when the bell rang, you ran, and you didn't care who you trampled over.

Much unlike the gentle part of you, that side was something to be feared. You were like a demon. In fact, during those times, I believe you were a demon, possessed by the substance you were after. Your whole life, the call of that altering substance, was stronger than any love, any life, or even God, your creator.

It eventually led you to a place where you could no longer fight. You wanted to rip things out, but you became weak, and that weakness cost you your life. A life that was full of torment and pain with little bits of sunshine in between, but as you said, the torment was stronger than the sun, and you were done.

The two lights and anchors of your life now being gone, there was nothing left to keep you here. Nothing left to make you want to turn around. Even when they were here, it was a challenge for you to stay well long enough to make it stick. With them now gone, it was over for you in your heart.

You wanted out, and when the heart wants something, eventually, in one way or another, it gets it. You led yourself to a place where your little body could no longer stand what was being done to it, and it was lights out.

You couldn't fight anymore. Gentle peace came over you as those you loved came to collect you and take you to a place where you no longer had to fight for that peace that you were looking for in your mind and heart. That rhythm you were looking for in your body. The rest from the striving.

That rest came for you to take you to a place where all of your tears would be wiped away and where your body could be made new. Your clothes be made white, and your face be wiped clean. Your heart restored to way beyond the womb, and you are now whole again.

With tears and sorrow, I sit here and mourn for you, but my eternal heart is joyful and hopeful for the day when I will see you again, in all of your eternal glory. The sunshine that I craved when you smiled will be eternal, and the tempest will remain in the grave.

You will wrap your arms around me, and you will laugh at me and with me, and we will have all eternity to form a new relationship which will not have these chainful bounds. We will finally be free to run in fields of gold… our own little Campo Dell'Oro.

What did I learn from you? To be true to the light that is within me. The light that shines brighter than the darkness. To follow that light. To resist the pull of the darkness and the rabbit trail of relentlessness that erases days and weeks, which turn into months and years.

To find the inner strength that pulls me through. To take the thoughts that are not mine and fend them off with the Word of Truth. To fight inside so that I don't have to fight on the outside. To make amends before things fester. To be of good cheer to everyone and let no one get the best of me. To find the common denominator in every situation that may be trying to take me down, and that sometimes, that common denominator is me, myself, with my unholy and unbridled thoughts of inadequacy that I let in myself. I let them through the portals and do not stop them at the gate. To find strength in every little thing I can so that I can hold myself up and keep going. To gently let go so peace can come.

You came in like a lion and went out like a lamb. Peace to you, my sweet and precious one.

33

CHAPTER 6

Navigating The Grief Finding Strength To Continue

Circumstances happen in life that make us wonder where God is in the midst of it all. Maybe you've asked yourself, "Where is God in my pain?" It can look as if all has gone dark and there is no one there to help you. The sun has gone down, the moon is not lighting your path, and you're left fumbling through the darkness.

For me, there was a lot going on all at once, and so many things and people to grieve that I started looking for the target on my back and forehead. I started wondering what I'd done to deserve all of these crazy ass things that were happening because in some instances, you just couldn't make this stuff ($#*!) up.

My life had become like a boxing ring, and the punches just kept coming. I was bruised, hurting, and tired. There were no more corners to run to, and ducking was no longer an option. The ring of life had me down for the count, and I in no way felt like a champion.

The list of disappointments, life struggles, and losses was so long it felt like there wasn't enough ink in my pens to write them all down. I started retreating into myself because I was tired of rehearsing failures and let-downs to those who asked how I was doing. I was lonely and in pain, but I tried to keep going with a smile on my face so no one could see what was really inside, because if they did, I felt they might just run away.

I'd like to say I handled my grief well in these past few years, but in hindsight, I'm not sure I did, especially in dealing with the culmination of all that happened throughout the pandemic and losing my brother. I let it all go, like one big sigh exhaling from my lungs and body.

Maybe you're familiar with this scenario... when you're wearing the painted-on skinny jeans to the big family get-together. You want to look good, so you wear them only to let the zipper down during the meal, and everything just falls out, but you're covered by your jumbo shirt? Thank goodness for those big shirts. They hide a multitude of sins and make us look good, even when that muffin top is all over the place underneath it! However, in the end, that muffin top has to go somewhere, and it's not going away just because it's covered.

That was me, coming apart like an unzipped tummy in real life, physically and emotionally. I was OK as long as I held it all in. Inside, I was bewildered, angry, and peaceful. Yes, all these emotions all at once and at varying times. From one side of the pendulum to the other, and I wasn't sure which side I'd be swinging from one moment to the next. Like David the Psalmist, I was swinging back and forth, hanging on to the rope with one hand and desperately grasping for God with the other.

Each loss that took place presented me with a unique way of grieving because of who they were, the depth of our relationship, and our experiences together. I'm no expert in the grieving process, unless all the losses I've experienced qualify me as one.

What I've learned is that despite the traditional grieving steps we're all familiar with and may try to follow, *there's no one specific or generic way to grieve for each person or thing we lose.*

Although there is a lot of helpful guidance out there, I had to remember that *grief, just like a fingerprint, is personal and individual.* There is no rule book or time frame. I can consult these processes, steps, acronyms, and tips, but nothing will stop the grief or shorten it. Biblically, we are advised to mourn for 30 days strongly and intentionally, and there are scripture references on how to mourn. I believe God put the time frame and processes in place so we wouldn't spend our lives grieving because there are serious repercussions to continuing in unhealthy grieving. In Proverbs 10:7, the Bible also states that their memory should be a blessing to us. So, we are to carry them with us in a healthy and loving manner.

We can take the helpful information that is out there and use it to help us in our process, keeping in mind that there is no foolproof way to check all the boxes, do all the steps, and you'll be done with it. The answers are also within us. Our spirits and bodies are guiding us and helping us through. These methods shouldn't be intended to keep us from or rush us through the grieving process.

It is a process. We have to acknowledge the loss and truly grieve in the best way for our individual selves in order for our souls to heal. It's not a one or two step and done deal. We can't think, "I'll walk through these specific steps, and I'll be healed." Even when I sat and just let my fingers type my feelings for my brother, it was a tremendous release, but alas, only temporary. There is more involved.

Reconciliation, time, love, prayer, and peace are required to fully heal. My hope is that you understand and know that you are not alone, and that the sharing of my vulnerable experiences and journal will help you in your grieving process.

In my healing process, I went uphill and then eventually downhill. I started off good, going uphill doing the work I thought was necessary, pacing myself, admiring the beautiful scenery, and taking it all in. Then it went downhill. I stopped doing what was helpful, and a little at a time, I drifted and started to tank fast. I allowed the spirit of grief to suck me in and forgot the Word of God because the pain of grief clouded everything. I was looking at my entire life through the lens of loss and pain. Any of you who wear glasses, even if they're sunglasses, know what it's like to try to get a clear picture when there's a smudge on the lenses. It's impossible. You've got to take measures to consistently clean them so you can see clearly.

CHAPTER 7

Building My Fortress

One bite at a time, I protected myself and built a wall around me. The comfort of that bite eventually built a fortress designed to protect me, which then became the wall that shut me in, and everything else out. Within those walls, shame, guilt, and disappointment grew, and I hid behind them in fear and for refuge. At times, if I'm not careful, I can go there again.

With each morsel, I gulped down my emotions, numbing myself, using food as a comfort tool to help me through. I had celebratory meal after celebratory meal, until I got to the point that I was sick, angry, disgusted, ashamed, and depressed. I couldn't believe that all the work I had put into reaching my goal weight had become undone. I had become undone. I was dealing with grief and family things that were hurtful, and I took it out on myself.

I was grieving the little things. Not being able to say goodbye. Not knowing how he was being treated, what was taking place, no updates, not knowing where they had put him. Seeing all the caskets lined up on Facebook all over the country was another excruciating reminder of what was taking place all around us.

How do we get him back and take him to where he should be laid to rest? Who's going to do that for us? How will it take place? Who do we reach out to? These are the things I thought about during the grieving process. Once all the prayers are answered and they are finally at rest, the necessary rest for those of us left behind doesn't come so easily. In this case, I saw it coming as I did with a few of them, and a few that surprised me, but they were all difficult in their own way.

Although I'm Christian, have a relationship with Jesus, the Holy Spirit as my guide, and the Word that I can turn to, it can be easy to get into the flesh and stay there for a while. When you're vulnerable, it's a piece of cake to lose control if you let yourself and then feel like you can't come back because of the guilt of going off track and not using the resources the Lord has given you.

I couldn't get a hold of myself. The more I gained, the more hopeless and depressed I became, and the further I got from others and into myself. A host of emotions stirred in my heart and mind. I wished I could have done things differently. I wondered if I could have done more for them. Stayed in closer contact, visited more often, answered those phone calls more frequently.

What I realized is that there is no way to go back other than through the lens of forgiveness. The only thing you can change now is how you feel and how you're going to move forward. Forgiving ourselves of our shortcomings and forgiving them for theirs, if need be, is necessary for healing. Holding on to things only keeps the heart, mind, and body in bondage, which means we are not free to live our lives in peace and victory.

Your situation is yours, and there's no one better than the Holy Spirit to help pull you through. God promises to never leave us or forsake us, so even in the middle of the most treacherous battle, He is with us. During this time, I got out a piece of paper, and I wrote my intentions for my brother. I brought them before the Lord, and as much as it hurt, it was good to look back and see how God answered.

There were times when it felt like there was such a long and deep silence from Him that it was almost deafening. Have you experienced this silence? You begin to wonder if God is there or not. Does He see your pain? Does He know you're hurting, and if He does, how long is He going to let it continue before He comes in, like that knight in shining armor, to rescue you and pull you from the wreckage?

I'm not sure if you're familiar with the story of the prodigal son in Luke 15, but I felt like him. I had an inheritance. I had taken it and forgot there was more available to me, and what it was really all about. This was about family, not money/inheritance. As portrayed in the story, it's about love, forgiveness, and redemption. I forgot the Word that says that I'm not without hope in this world. I started living with the pigs and began thinking that this was my lot in life and all that I deserved until one day I came to my senses and decided to walk back home to that family and under the covering within that home.

There have been many losses in my life. From my earlier years, I've lost dear ones, one after the other. They each had their own special place in my life and heart, and I learned wonderful lessons from each of them.

Sometimes you see their end coming, and at times, it comes out of left field. It can make sense or take you totally off guard. It's in those times when I was caught off guard that grieving for me was more difficult. Even in losing special loved ones, the ones that seemed senseless were the worst.

Grieving for the ones that shock you to the core, like a terrible scene from a bad dream you can't wake up from, can be challenging and heart-wrenching to process. Coming back from these can take a little longer, and even when you feel like you've turned a corner, a new wave rushes over you and knocks you on your hiney into the sand.

I've seen people express their grief in so many ways. You just never knew what someone was going to do when we went to a funeral. I'm not trying to mock the grieving process, but growing up Italian, things were a little different. I've even seen people jumping into a beloved's grave because of their immense grief.

We can be intense or have so many things take place in a short period of time that we become indifferent… like another one biting the dust. As time goes by, there have been so many losses that you become numb and matter-of-fact to what is happening and who has passed away.

I remember a time not too long ago when we lost 18 people in a 17-month period. Some of them were very close to me. My father being one of them. A couple of very dear best friends. Strong presences in my life. It just seemed like people were graduating to their heavenly home, expiring left and right, and, as mentioned, a handful of them were key people in life.

These changes in our lives can be intense. Some of the people we lose could be the very ones who have the most dirt on us and were our go-to's when we couldn't go to anyone else. These souls kept our deepest and darkest secrets in their hearts, and now their hearts have stopped beating, and they've taken the secrets with them.

Be kind to yourself, give yourself time, and seek the help you need. The help we seek must be curtailed to us and instrumental in our healing process for us individually, as everyone grieves differently. I've noticed that with my experiences and in people I have lost, and even as I help others through their grieving process that this is a necessary and crucial process, for our ultimate healing.

Some things I did to help me grieve were to give each person I had lost the honor they deserved in my life. I would think of the unique things that made them who they were and their special place in my life. Each one had something they brought to my life that was a lesson and a memory that I treasure that will carry me through and provide strength in times of need.

I kept their memory alive in my life and as a blessing to those around me by remembering and recounting how they made their mark in my life, how they loved me, the deposits they made in me that changed me forever. I thought about the invaluable lessons they taught me that I could pass on to others to help them in their daily walk. Taking these special steps provided me with peace and comfort.

Years ago, the family unit was very different than it is now. We had close aunts, uncles, cousins, and extended family members who passed on precious stories of those in our lives. I feel that has somehow been compromised. It could be our distance from each other. Although the internet has provided ways of keeping us closer.

We don't share and keep people in remembrance like we used to. We don't pass on the wonderful experiences and memories that made their lives precious and left a mark on all of us. It seems like people are evaporating off the face of the earth, and unless they accomplished something and their name is somewhere, they are nowhere. Let's let them live on in our hearts while we grieve them. Let's tell others about them when it's prudent and necessary so that others hear wonderful stories of those who have gone before us.

What legacy will you leave behind? We do have a choice in this matter.

Grief doesn't know time… it can show up today, tomorrow, or in a few years.

If you have lost your grip on your grieving and need help on your journey, please reach out.

CHAPTER 8

The Development Of The Pandemic Brain

Since the pandemic, many aspects of our lives have drastically changed or ceased to exist. We had months of inactivity, anxiety, and uncertainty. We've had some issues with uncertainty in life and these uncertainties have caused us to doubt, lose faith in what we've held dear, and tamper with our trust.

Our routines have been disrupted, our communities have been diluted, and social interaction has decreased, if not totally ceased. We've been forced to adapt to new 'normals' that can disrupt our peace and sense of well-being. We've become apathetic, tired, and depressed. We are no longer social, and we've resorted to unhealthy coping mechanisms.

These months of uncertainty have led to cognitive impairment and caused our brains to be less agile and in a state of fog. We may even have difficulty remembering specifics. Have you experienced symptoms of confusion, inability to remain focused, forgetfulness, indecisiveness, or mild to deep depression? You are not alone.

Brain fog can be caused by stress, anxiety, lack of sleep, an unhealthy diet, and changes in hormones. You can improve your symptoms by eating a healthy diet, exercising regularly, and optimizing your mental health.

For me, it also felt as if the progress in my life came to a halt, which caused disconnection and, at times, inexplicable pain. Have you ever felt pain? Just all over, no particular place, just everywhere, like a cold chill that you can't get rid of? What I've learned is that despite feeling like this, there is a way out. Our bodies and minds are so resilient and, they are great adapters.

Movement is the brain's best friend. Being mobile, exercising, and cognitively working on triggers like stress and grief help us to raise our serotonin levels and relieve some of the pain we're experiencing. We can also put systems in place that can set us up for success.

Trauma can make or break us if we let it. The upside to this is that we can turn it around to foster resilience and triumph. With proper, strategic, and intentional approaches, we can be victorious in life. Because of the magnificence of the neuroplasticity of our minds, we can stretch and return, much like a rubber band, coming back stronger and better. We can break free of this pain and suffering.

As we change our thoughts, we change our realities… so make sure that the reality you are rehearsing in your mind is the one you want. Retrain your mind to think on the things that are good, wholesome, and worthy. (Philippians 4:8)

What gets measured gets managed. If you're continually and consistently checking in on yourself, there's less of a chance that things will fall through the proverbial cracks. Especially when you're honest with yourself. Daily, weekly, and monthly progress check-ins are so helpful and critical to our well-being. They help us to stay on the track of wholeness.

I've been getting back in the habit of regular check-ins right after I do something that causes my heart to go dark. I try not to let it fester for too long. The Bible teaches me that I'm not supposed to go to bed angry, which to me means that there is a moratorium on our not-so-stellar behavior before there are mental, emotional, and physical repercussions. That looks to me like a 12-hour period at most.

It's great to unload everything and leave it at the foot of The Throne. I remember one day in particular, going to bed and just having all this stuff. There was so much that it felt like a garbage bag on my back. I walked into The Throne Room, and I dumped that huge bag on the right side of God's Throne. I jumped into His lap and put my head on His chest. I just wanted to let it all go and have Him love me, forgive me, and help me with everything that was in that ugly black bag.

The next day, I went to the funeral of a friend's dad. The man was a well-revered Christian doctor who had pastors as his closest friends. One of them got up and began sharing cherished memories of his dear friend. He talked about how we should take all of our burdens, especially this burden of grief, to the Lord. His eyes started to tear as he described how grateful he was that he was able to do this and encouraged us to do the same. I was in awe! He was describing my dream!!!

Shocker! I'd never met this man, and yet, he was describing exactly what I had seen. During our repast time, I went over and asked if I could sit next to him. I thanked him for sharing his memory and told him of my vision. He shared that he had been reluctant to share that particular thing and was glad that the Lord confirmed his desire to share it through me. Tears came to both of our eyes as we saw how the Lord was in our grief and pain and had used us to help heal the other.

What's the point? God sees everything, and He sees YOU. He loves you and wants to unload that burden you've put on your back. If you're hurting over the loss of your family, friends, and things you've held dear, no one is more familiar with your pain than Him, and He will help you to heal from that pain and overcome. AND... He will send whomever He sees would be fittest to help us through that healing process.

HE SEES YOU!

CHAPTER 9

I.C.U.
I See YOU

Many people are walking around bleeding. They are guarded so you cannot see the bleeding, but it's there. They're hurting and need triage. They need help, and they are afraid to ask for it. They want to stay anonymous about their pain and still be seen.

They want the respect that's due them because of the pain that they've experienced. They want to be recompensed for the sadness, hurt, and stabbings that have taken place over and over again in their lives. Their pain was significant. It should be worth something. The suffering has to count for something.

Recently, I had a very vivid dream just as I was waking up. In my dream, I was in a small grocery store where I picked up a couple of items and proceeded to the checkout. A gentle Asian woman in a black coat got there before me. I watched as she placed her items on the counter and slid them closer to the cashier.

She rang up the items and gave her the total. The woman looked at her in dismay… as if the total was incorrect. "Isn't there a discount?" she asked, "I've been through so much; I should get a discount." It was as if the cashier was looking right through her, not seeing her pain and not understanding why she would be eligible for a discount.

The woman, still confused, turned to me. I was on her right side, and a tear gently rolled down her cheek. I could see the pain behind her eyes as she reached out to me with them, silently and tearfully asking me for help. I was familiar with that pain. I knew what she meant. She wanted recompense for all the pain she had experienced in life. For her broken pieces to count for something. For her cracks to be filled with gold. For those broken pieces to matter.

I leaned in and gave her a long, strong hug in hopes of letting her know I understood. I got her. That hug represented both of our journeys. I knew her because I was her. In that hug, I attempted to communicate that I saw her, that she mattered, that she counted, and I knew her pain. With that hug of understanding, I was able to comfort her and bring her peace.

We pulled back from our embrace, and she said, "I want to take you somewhere. Will you please come with me?" She extended her hand, so I offered mine, and she proceeded to guide me to different places in her life. She introduced me to her friends and family, and as we walked along, she asked them to come meet the woman who had helped her. She then went on to recount what had happened to her and kept saying, "She's my friend, she helped me, she understands me."

Funny thing about this dream. Just a few days before, I was looking into the ancient Japanese art of Kintsugi. The meaning or translation of the word is 'join with gold.' This is a method of repairing ceramics and glass with gold in order to restore them and make them stronger so they can be used again.

This practice reminded me that Jesus wants to heal us, to fix those broken places, restoring them, making them whole by filling them with gold, thus making them stronger and more precious than they were before.

The Word says that the Lord makes everything beautiful in its own time and His power is made perfect in the places where we are weak. Ecclesiastes 3:11 and 2 Corinthians 12:19, respectively. (Emphasis mine).

Embracing our scars and imperfections and giving them to the Lord results in something more beautiful and valuable in the end. God sees us and loves us. Do we see each other? Do we look beyond what's going on in our lives just long enough to see the pain in their eyes and the reservations in those around us? Their pull back and retreat for fear of being hurt, judged, or gossiped about by sharing their pain?

Who has God brought into your life who may need help or to help you with the pain you're going through? We need to see each other, to acknowledge our pain, talk about it and bring comfort to each other, for we are Jesus' hands here on earth.

If you're exhausted from living in a physical or mental prison, isn't it time you get the help you deserve?

Look back over the past 10 years. What mattered most to you? What choices were you presented with that you feel you handled well, and which ones do you wish you had handled differently? Let God fill those broken and cracked places with gold.

CHAPTER 10

Stay Proactive
Anticipate Tomorrow

To see results in any area, consistency is the name of the game. Get ahead of "IT" before "IT" gets ahead of you. Staying on top of it and maintaining the win before it becomes a loss. No pun intended. When I checked in on myself on a regular basis, it was easy to see where I was falling short, and the correction was easier.

When I let my ship get miles off course, without checking the compass or being aware of my surroundings, was when it was most difficult to regain my bearings and see where I was and start moving the rudder in the right direction again.

Our plans and desires, the reasons why we're doing things, have to be louder than the cloudiness and head stuff that goes on in our minds. We have to remember to stay cognizant of why we're doing this and realize that while some things are good rewards, others are not. It's not a good practice to keep rewarding yourself with food when you reach one of your milestones. It's better to buy a new shirt or find another marker that helps you celebrate without the possibility of harm to your mind or body. If it's going to set you back and make it longer to reach your goal, put it down! I use self-care as one of my rewards. I'll use special treatments such as a mask, cleanser, bath salt, new shampoo, lip color, or something that is going to hug my body and thank it for helping me reach this milestone.

They don't call them SMART goals for nothing! In this case, not only must our goals be smart, but we must also be smart in executing them. If you're unfamiliar with SMART goals, they are simple, measurable, achievable, relevant, and time-bound.

What is the best weight goal for you right now? Make it simple, just focus on a small portion of the weight you can manage now. Look at the next 5 or 10 pounds instead of looking at the whole total of weight you want to shed.

Embarking on any journey, you're given a roadmap. You don't see the whole road in one fell swoop as you're traveling. You only see bits of the road at a time, as far as your eyes can see in that moment. Go that far. Never mind the twists and turns and the miles ahead, just keep going, and when you get *there*, you'll deal with each pound shed as it presents itself.

Put it in proper perspective so that little by little it can be achieved. Measure how long it will take and allow yourself a little wiggle room. Be very realistic as to how much time you will give yourself. None of us wants to crash and burn and be faced with the disappointments that can come through unrealistic goal setting. Celebrate even the smallest of achievements so you have a memory of the win to carry you through to further and greater victory.

How relevant to your life is the process of reaching this goal? Why are you doing this now, and draw out your *WHY*. Make it fit in with the rest of life, as this is a journey and not a destination. Things will come on your path that are part of your life... fold this into it. You are part of it, and it is part of you.

We measure life in years, months, weeks, days, and moments. So, knowing that, do what is best for you. Since this is a journey, we must prepare ourselves for life events. Putting plans in place, we can honor these things and approach them in a healthy manner so that they don't derail us.

Let's face it, Holidays are inevitable, weddings and special occasions will take place. They are also part of our journey in life. They are meant for celebration, not a place to gorge and stuff our feelings or avoid interaction with others. Eat your fun foods, enjoy people, and get back on when it's over. If you're prepared mentally and physically for them, they will be easier to manage when you see a couple of extra pounds on the scale. I chose to just start despite the fact that there was a trip and a wedding in the month

I was starting. I looked at the whole month and decided that these 4 days weren't going to outweigh the other 27. I did what I wanted and what was necessary for me to be present and enjoy my surroundings. Then, I just went right back to my plan after the celebrations.

Allow yourself to have fun if something is coming up that is going to slightly alter your path. Resolve to either eat what is there, enjoying your once-in-a while favorites, and then get right back on as soon as the event is over. Or, prepare yourself beforehand if possible, and adjust and compensate for what you're going to face, so you can stick to your plan without feeling left out. Like eating beforehand, going there for the fellowship and social benefits instead of the food.

I have looked at events such a wedding as special moments that only come once in a lifetime. I am going to enjoy myself and eat what I want, and tomorrow, I will get right back to my eating plan, maybe even making some restitution, such as a light detox, like drinking extra water or tea and having more greens to help flush things out. Or, I will just eat a little of all that's presented to me. I will just eat to nourish my body and taste a little of what looks good to me, and continue engaging in conversation. There's more to an event than food. I don't have to act like a binge eater, thinking that I'd better eat this now because I may never eat this again.

Which brings me to another point. It's not a good or bad girl thing. On its own, food is what it is. The way we look at it, the value we place on it, and what it means to us are what change its definition, relevance, and purpose. How we think of it and use it is what gives it the power that it has on our minds and lives.

We cannot think to ourselves that we're going to eat this whole box and we're never buying this again (unless it's really gross 😄). That is a myth and not realistic. That is a binge and purge, all-or-nothing attitude. We want to come from a healthy mentality where there is balance and peace. We're eating whatever it is because we're physically hungry, because we like it and want to try it. To give ourselves nourishment or a treat, not to stuff down the feelings we don't want to deal with.

Food is nourishment. We must look at it in the same way we look at purchasing fuel for our cars to run on. Cars do not run without fuel. Devices do not work unless charged. The same is true for our bodies. Food is fuel for our bodies.

I remember when I was in corporate, one of my tasks as the office admin and manager was to process expense reports. One day, one of our executives handed hers in. It was my first time processing her expense report. She was a wonderful woman from Europe, very tall and thin. For the food portion of it, she called her meals sustenance. Everyone else, who was pretty much born stateside, called them food or meals. I had never seen food classified as sustenance. A new perspective on food lit up in my mind like a 100-watt bulb. Food was there to sustain me.

Growing up Italian, food meant many things. You're not feeling well? Let's have some food. You're hungry? Let's have some food. Someone is coming over? Let's make some food. We're going to someone's house? Let's bring some food. Somebody died? Let's make them some food. You weigh less than XX pounds? Let's give you some food and put meat on those bones. Do you see where I'm going?? 😆

Although there are Biblical instances when food was for purposes other than sustenance, its primary role was to provide energy for people to complete their daily tasks. Once in a while, it was used for feasts, and the Word says that the Lord wanted them to have rich foods to celebrate those occasions, but it doesn't go into all these crazy things I grew up with. I say this to say that there has been a gross distortion as to what food is or is not for us. A value has been placed on it, not of our own doing. Food is and should be our sustenance, not something we turn to in order to deal with our emotions.

As we become more sedentary as a society, it's important to stay mobile through exercise, physically and mentally. There are so many things out there to help us, but I think in some ways, it has made us lazier, having to do less and less ourselves. We have to find the balance between help and hindrance. If something, like technology, is doing something more for you than you are doing for yourself, it's good to give it a second look.

Helpers are designed to help us, not hinder us, and keep us from using our own minds and bodies to complete the work that's been outlined for us throughout our days. Having them around to help us is great, but when our reliance on them is greater than our reliance on God and the gifts He's deposited within us, it's time to take a second look to see if that "thing" we've come to rely on is helping us to be the best selves we've been called to be.

So… get your exercise in… mentally and physically. Take those extra steps to give your body a little more movement. Do some thinking that will stretch your mind. Get yourself out of the "do it for me" box and do some things for yourself that will optimize your well-being and cause it to soar.

CHAPTER 11

The Shadow Of Repetition
The Fear And Trauma
Of Doing It Again

Have you lost your place in life? I have. Many times. You were going along, and all was well, and then you got blindsided by something you never saw coming. Maybe you did see it coming, but as words that sometimes escape from our mouths that we want to take back as soon as they're released, that's how life is sometimes. You can't grab it back and keep it from getting out there. Once the arrow is released, it's on its way to its target, and it will eventually hit something.

I've fallen hard! Have you ever fallen so hard that you're not sure if you can or want to get back up again? Maybe, like me, you're afraid that if you do get up, you'll only get so far and then you'll fall flat on your face. You either don't trust yourself or those around you to help you get to where you were. I was so disappointed in myself for making decisions that harmed my temple. I was constantly apologizing to myself and the Holy Spirit for the sabotage and repercussions I'd caused to my body, mind, and spirit.

The enemy has a way of planting mental seeds of the grass being greener on the other side. He bombards you with thoughts that make you want to leave the paradise you're in because you see that grass across the street more clearly than the blessings that are right in front of you. Let me tell you from experience that the minute you put one toe, let alone your foot, on that greener grass, it will turn brown right before your eyes and suck you in. The enemy of our souls then uses those very temptations we've acted on to condemn us for the decision he bombarded us to make.

You listen, you go against what you know to be true in your heart, and immediately the condemnation rises. It attacks your mind, heart, and spirit. It makes you feel horrible and then he starts bombarding you with self-loathing in attempts to make you feel bad for going down the road he intended you to take in the first place. His M.O. is to get you to listen, cross over that line, and then shame you for it.

My experience has been that there are two reasons for the barrage that comes fast and furious. First, to draw us in, and second, to hinder our physical and spiritual growth. It comes on hard, so we'll do it quickly, without thinking, and fall into sin. Once we're on the ground, he makes us feel guilty. That shame temporarily distances us and breaks fellowship with the Holy Spirit. This is an attempt to rob us of the blessing God has waiting right around the corner. Whenever there's a big blessing coming, he's right there to try and stop it by setting the stage for a fall. However, one word, one step towards forgiveness, will remedy that distance in less than a heartbeat. As we draw close to God and confess our sins, the Lord will honor His Word and forgive us, and because of Jesus's sacrifice, we are in right standing again.

I'm still not in the place where I feel I'm fully winning in my heart. I'm maintaining, but the break I need in my mind to move forward in a way that I'd like has not completely happened yet. I am still not in the "ZONE" that I'd like to be in to get back to my sweet spot, and honestly, I'm not sure what it's going to take to make the switch in my brain to make that happen.

Part of me is scared that I'll just keep doing this for the rest of my life, so why put myself through the pain again? As another milestone birthday draws near, I think of the latter part of my life. Although I've been proclaiming that my latter years are going to be better than my former years, honestly, at the moment, I don't see it in this area of my life.

I keep looking back to patterns of loss and gain. For example, I get to that place where I want to be, and then this imposter syndrome takes over. Something in me tells me I don't belong here, that this is not for me. The questions start, and the voices begin. Why are you here?? You don't belong here. This is not your territory. You are not one of the thin ones in life. You don't fit in and don't deserve to be here. I am, however, hopeful as I make progress on a smaller scale until the intensity rises again.

Somehow, you've told yourself that this is not for you. It's like you're walking forward on your new path, and your past self pulls at your shirt from behind so your future self can't move forward.

Maybe it's time to pump up the volume to drown out the punk of your soul! Drown the voices out with music and the Word so you can move forward. What have you used before to get your groove back? Can you use that same method again to jumpstart this new journey?

CHAPTER 12

Loosening My Grip
The Summer Of Me

I lost it, then I gained it. There are many reasons why this happened... grief, pain, uncertainty, but most of all, I felt like there was something in my brain that just wouldn't shut off my mouth. I couldn't get myself to say 'yes' to health and 'no' to the food that was in front of me or the treats that came to mind that I wanted to sample, or to eat.

I denied myself nothing, as it says in the Bible about Solomon, the wisest and richest king on earth, who eventually came to his ruin. He went from being revered by God and man to being a depraved pagan womanizer, abandoning his relationship with God for his depravities.

When you live that way, you go down paths that take you places you didn't mean to go. At the time, that path was alluring. Now faced with the consequences at the end of the line, in your heart of hearts, you realize that you never wanted it to get that far.

Every once in a while, when I fall short of the Word of God, I joke around and say that it was an episode of spiritual amnesia. Are you like an amnesia patient that doesn't remember what needs to be remembered, but you can recall the stupidest of things that have no bearing on how you're going to get your best help now?

Are you so immobilized by grief, trauma, and pain that you cannot move? Like you've been shot up with one of those neuromuscular blocking agents on TV, and you're paralyzed? You're alive, you can think and see everything around you, but you cannot move to take the action or actions necessary to get out or get help?

Grief and trauma can do that to you. You're living in an alternate reality and universe, behind an imaginary glass. Your mind is scattered in so many places that it cannot follow one simultaneous thought. You're alive and breathing, but you're not really here.

I saw in my mind, through the Holy Spirit, that I needed to refrain from being in strife with my own body. Just as the scriptures talk about strife and how unhealthy it is to remain in it, so it is with us. I recently saw a commercial where two identical men were fighting, and it was symbolic of the fight we have within. I believe that when we fight ourselves, it is not good for our overall well-being.

I'm staring in the mirror, putting on my makeup. I'm thinking of what shirt I'm going to wear for Thanksgiving. I'm annoyed that nothing I have fits me, not because I'm close to my highest weight ever, planning not to get there, but because I gave all my "fat" clothes away with no intention of coming back to this place.

As previously mentioned, I aced the pandemic. I went to bed early to keep my circadian rhythm in check. I'd wake up earlier to start my day with a good workout. I took a shower and put on clean jammies... come on, laugh with me, I know you did it too. 😂

I took care of things that needed to be taken care of in the household. I ate well. I didn't allow myself to go nuts and eat like crazy as a means of coping with the uncertainty that was all around me. I used my inside power girl to find ways to keep my body and mind in check.

And then it happened. I lost track of my brother, who was overseas, and the next thing we knew, he was dead. With the way things were run in that area, it felt like I was dealing with a third-world country. Then we had a family event that ended in a blowup, which totally messed with my head. Then we had more Holidays, and the party continued. Soon after, one of my best friends passed away, and then my brother-in-law, and the spiral continued.

I was so frustrated, embarrassed, and angry with myself! Yet, that didn't stop me. No, I continued in the madness of eating more than my body needed. When I'd get on the scale, I would think... it's not that bad, it's been worse, and I would walk away, watch for a little, but then start again and continue on in my depravity.

The pain of what it took to get within 10 pounds of my goal weight, only to gain it back, was excruciating. Then, I had to stop working out because of an injury. All the work that went into that, all the "dieting," making new recipes, gaining 5 and losing 5, staying at a stalemate for weeks but pushing through for breakthrough, kept appearing like little flashbacks in my mind. The trauma of having gone through that only to gain it back was too much of a shock to put myself back in the game and try again. I was disillusioned, defeated, and distraught for where I was now and was mourning where I was before. I wanted that me and that time back.

CHAPTER 13

Snack Nation

I want to start out by saying that I believe in a 5-meal-a-day eating plan… 3 traditional meals… breakfast, lunch, and dinner, with one or two snacks in between.

My journey has not been easy, but in comparison to most, it may look that way. Since I can remember, I have had a certain relationship with food that to this day I am not sure that I can define properly. I don't know if it is an addiction or maybe just still trying to find my path on how to take care of my body with the very thing that brings me joy, yet adds to me in a way that I do not like.

The things and places that were a special treat on certain celebratory occasions have turned into daily staples or quick ways to eat, using those places and meals, if you want to call them that, to replace proper planning. Instead of creating a meal plan, taking a little time to shop for what's needed, make it beforehand, and having the food ready to eat, we leave ourselves open, with no plan, which leads to less than perfect choices.

This lack of vision and planning leaves you with more consequences because we eventually end up getting something fast. Then, we're left with malnutrition, not having the micronutrients to produce proper energy, and we increase our fat mass capacity and decrease our energy levels. Those unhealthy items we choose can also be addictive, as many additives and preservatives are, and we end up wanting more because of the emptiness and lack of satisfaction.

I came from a place where the soil was rich the food was wholesome. We had breakfast, lunch, dinner, and a snack before dinner. The snacks were usually pretty healthy, and even if they deviated a little, they were still made with fairly wholesome ingredients. Unfortunately, my homeland has been inundated with unhealthy and empty foods now as well, and their levels of overweightedness are climbing too.

I would go back and forth to visit family, and the minute I was stateside, the weight started piling on. I know that stress and a change of environment had something to do with that. I also know this, coupled with a lack of mobility, had a play in it, but food had the biggest impact. Every time I went back, I would lose weight quickly. I even had blood tests that showed all was well, and my pediatrician from birth labeled it as an allergy to additives and preservatives, which cause bloating.

I ate foods that were minimally processed. I enjoyed snacking. I liked having treats. My American counterparts seemed to eat everything they wanted and never gained weight. How I wanted to be like them. It looked like a privilege to be able to eat stuff like that and have it be a little treat, something that made me feel better. Unfortunately for me, I would only get momentary reprieve because within minutes after eating the treats, my body would start going nuts. I would start to feel the drop in my blood sugar, the stress on my body, and it was a bloating feeling that left me restless, tired, and with no energy. A snack that is supposed to hold you over and help you feel better between meals was starting to feel like it had no purpose, other than piling up more weight on my little body and making me sick.

I would binge, and after those feelings came over me, I would purge because I wanted it out of my system quickly, so it would not have that effect on me physically, emotionally, and weight wise. Skipping a meal, extra workouts, lots of water and some veggies or salads were my favorite ways to purge.

So, throughout my years, I was heavy, then thin, then heavy, then thin. Always going back and forth with little control. I tried many different diets and would lose the weight, only to gain it right back, or at least a good portion of it.

CHAPTER 14

Just Say NO To Self-Sabotage

Are you self-sabotaging? Is something big coming up, and you're not sure how to handle it, so you are stress-eating? Do you not know how to handle it? Do you think you can't trust yourself to finish what you started?

Do you think or feel you can't come through for yourself, so you turn to food to make yourself fail, and blame it on something else?

Is your mindset that you fail anyway, and you're so used to failing that you don't even try?

Going back in memories and life, I see a pattern of addiction. Whether it's alcohol, drugs, or food. Some people don't think food is an addiction, but in my case, sometimes I do. Like other addictions, this one is different. Alcohol, drugs, or pills are not necessary to sustain life. Food is. You need it to survive, and it's everywhere. It's the most common, accepted, and available form of drug... at least for those of us who look or may use it that way.

Hear me out, I have to make myself think of it as fuel for my body, not something I can take to make me feel better, drown out my feelings, deal with something I don't want to deal with, a procrastination propeller, whether it's family, business, or just life.

Growing up, I saw a few family members deal with this sort of thing, in all facets of the spectrums mentioned above. The ones that were food related were more peculiar to me than the others. They were the hiders, there one minute and gone the next. Disappearing for periods of time and then resurfacing, only allowing you to see certain parts of them at certain times. They were flatlined, up or down, like Jeckles and Hydes. You never knew which one you were going to get. I missed those people dearly. I missed them when they hid because I lost out on the opportunity to have conversations and share life with them.

At this stage of my life, I'm doing it myself. I've retreated for different reasons. Most of them are so that I don't get hurt as I'm following a specific path to change things in my life. Some people get excited for you when you share. They cheer you on and support you in any way they can. While others don't want you to change because perhaps the changes you are making are placing a spotlight on and magnifying things they are struggling to change. Maybe they see things in themselves that they're afraid to change or don't have the strength or desire to change.

I remember throughout my life that when I wanted to change myself, my body, my life, there were people who, in their own way, opposed the changes I wanted to make and the future I wanted to move toward. Blessed souls telling me that I couldn't do certain things, make a certain amount of money, or you're getting too thin, when all you're doing is wanting to live a healthy, prosperous life and feel good about yourself.

You don't live my life, and you're not in my body. Who are you to tell me that I'm getting too thin? Do you even know me? I've never been "too thin" in my entire life. There's always been a pooch, a fat arm, or a bit more cheek and chin than I'd like.

People sculpt themselves every day... why can't I do that for myself? Did anyone ever tell Arnold, Lou, or Sylvester to their faces that they were getting too muscular? I'm sure. Mostly, though, I think they admired them for their resolve. Why can't they admire us for ours? Why can't they just understand that we're not comfortable and want to make a change? Why can't they understand that when we look in the mirror, we don't like what we're seeing at the moment and want to implement the necessary steps toward facilitating those changes? Why don't they understand that we want to shed the extra because we feel trapped?

If you've never been in that way in your mind, spirit, or body, then please don't judge those who are struggling. The struggle is for a reason, and we need to deal with that struggle. How we deal with it, although personal, must be done in a healthy manner. It doesn't matter if you come out the other end a size 4 when your insides, your brain, hair, and everything in you have been so depleted due to improper nutrition that now you have bigger issues to deal with.

I don't remember going through this when I was younger. I don't remember being this conscious or needing to watch my food intake when I was in my home country. I don't recall my mind and body changing until we moved here to the States. I'm not sure if it was the bullying at school or something else. All I know is that I started off thin in the second grade and by the time third grade came around, I was a bloated little porker. I'm not sure how I got there, what I went through mentally, emotionally, or physically, but when I look at my school pictures, I see that there are changes, and those changes continued into my middle school years.

I also grew up faster physically than those around me. My period came sooner; boobies came sooner. I remember one year when we went back to Italy for the summer, my Mom took me to my pediatrician, and they ran tests. I don't remember for what, and there's no one I could ask now, but I do remember my Mom saying she didn't understand what happened to me. It seemed like when we got to the U.S., I quickly gained weight, and then when we came to Italy, I would lose it all again. The pediatrician said he thought it was because of the additives and preservatives in the American diet. Was he on to something all those years ago?

Not sure how you all handle stuff, but my body doesn't like anything that's artificial, all jacked up with sugar or other things outside of its natural nature. I see people enjoy hot chocolate, sweets, and other "treats," and my body goes on a rampage when I have them. Nothing ever tastes as good as it looks, and my body never feels the same after I have them. I cannot really enjoy a piece of cake, cookie, or whatever because I know what's coming afterwards. Dizziness, sleepiness, sluggishness, feeling like my mind and body are going to shut down. Then I want something salty or a big cup of coffee to counteract it, so it piles up.

When I was old enough, I started going off on my own. I couldn't do that before for certain reasons, mainly the way I grew up, which is a whole other story. Anywho, in my second year of high school, I decided I was going to change some things. I remember drinking a lot of iced tea and doing yoga in my hot room without A/C (I wish I had thought of hot yoga). I think I lost about 20 pounds by the time the summer was over. This was a different "Summer of Me." When I went back to school, some people were a little shocked when they saw me, and it felt good to experience the new, comfortable, confident me. What they thought didn't matter, because I was good with how I looked and felt.

I started subscribing to things like health magazines to help myself, and a new desire surfaced within me. I realized that with exercise, my body felt different, and I liked how it felt. I liked how my mind felt. How much sharper it was, and the independence that I felt.

I wanted others who were like me to experience the same thing... this freedom inside. I wanted them to be free in their bodies, no matter how much they weighed, because we all know there is freedom and comfort in the acceptance of our own beings.

The power of remembrance. When things come at us, why is it a challenge to remember how we're feeling right now? The strength we have inside, the resolve we've made to live well. Something happens, and we lose the power, become listless, and give in to the emotions. My experience has been that when I lose that perspective, I lose the power. When I lose the power, then I lose myself. Then what I'm left with is two things... the problem didn't go away because I didn't deal with it, I stuffed it under the rug of food, and now I have the extra weight to deal with. Along with this also come the feelings of wanting to hurt myself. The way my body feels when I've gone off the rails is there... the headaches, the nausea, the poison in my body, the weight gain. So, remembering the consequences sometimes stops me from dealing with situations in an unhealthy manner, or by taking them out on myself.

Most of the time, I remember. Especially during the pandemic, I remembered every day. However, when the losses started to happen and the disappointments of the surrounding situations, especially with regard to the situation with my brother, I forgot. One meal at a time, I forgot. One workout at a time, I forgot, and I just let it pile up. I was miserable, trapped in my own skin. Not understanding why I was allowing this, doing the woe is me, not understanding why things happen in life the way they do.

I became angry; I became powerless. Missing people in my life who meant so much to me. Having to deal with things on my own now, without their craziness or their joy in my life. One thing I realized as I looked back was that they had had enough. Almost every single one of them decided to let go in their own way. That was hard for me to accept.

I remember seeing my best friend spiral down. Going from being a believer to eventually not wanting to go out of the house. Giving in to things that she knew were going to make her life miserable, but the depression that comes from not seeing change can lead us down dark and destructive paths.

We go to the familiar; we wallow there, and we don't move because we're paralyzed. Shaking ourselves to wake up from that nightmare can be the greatest thing we can do for ourselves. Staying in a state of unconsciousness keeps us in the dark, listless, powerless, numb, and without the strength to fight.

Is everything going to be great every day? Nope, get that in your head before you start. I had to drill it in. However, we need the necessary tools to deal with those days when they come. We need purpose and things bigger than we are to look forward to in order to shrink the things that could come for our lives and all that is dear to them. When those things try to come for our dreams, it's important that the dream is bigger than the thing that is coming for us.

In some circles, it's called your WHY. If your WHY isn't bigger than the situation that's going on now, you will crumble under the pressure of it all. Make your WHY visible wherever you are, so you don't lose sight of it when things aren't flowing your way.

My eyes got fuzzy. The struggle of getting to where I wanted to be caused so much stress in my life. Mainly, because people didn't like where I was and where I was headed. Every time they saw me, they would comment on how thin I was getting. They saw the weight, the thinness, not the emotional and mental progress that was taking place inside me. They didn't stop to ask questions or see beyond the shrinking. Maybe for their own selfish purposes, they didn't want to. You know how it is sometimes. You ask questions when you want the change, but you stay silent if you're afraid you can't make the changes you want to make yourself. I was taking care of and managing what was important to me. I was getting down to my goal on my terms. Every once in a while, I would hear the words of my doctor. Now I'm older, and this is a loftier goal for a woman my age.

Sometimes, when we get close, there's someone pulling us from our shirttails… they're bringing us back to reality… but whose reality is it? Theirs?

They're trying to bring us down. The lyrics to an extremely popular song are in my mind when I think of how to respond to them... hey, you, get off of my cloud. Let me be who I am. Trust that I'm dealing with stuff, and what you think doesn't matter. Only my journey with God matters.

So, it started with the family event. Then it was Thanksgiving, and though I'm a celebrator, people around me weren't celebrating. They didn't want to. We were in waiting mode to see what other people were doing, and it was causing me turmoil inside. Some things close ones do can make you feel horrible, and they don't know it. Extended family can cause issues through their actions or inactions. Unexplained sabotages of time can be frustrating, and after years of waiting, I decided that the following year I was going to continue in the way that I was used to before. I was going to make plans because why mourn those who don't want to be with you when there are others who want to spend time with you and value you so much that they will change their plans to be with you because that's how much you matter to them.

You've had an impact on their lives and despite your little quirks, they enjoy what's in you and who God created you to be.

At the beginning of December, I learned of the passing of my brother. I received a call from a less than pleasant family member who thought the news of my brother's death was a fun message to deliver. Have you ever had those people in your life? They want bad news for you because they're so miserable themselves?

That news started over a month of questions. Because he was in another country, it was difficult to get help needed to find out the circumstances surrounding his death. You know the language, but you can't get answers. It's like nobody knows what's going on. Nobody knows where, what, how, or why, and as someone who needs details, statistics, etc., that is a hard pill to swallow. We were so grateful for the little information and help we were able to get.

God answered my prayers for dignity in his handling. He also answered prayers for His goodness to shine forth. Despite the huge delay, the Lord was working things out in me and around me, and the victory and details He worked out gave Him all the glory. It was a very stressful and frustrating time period. Talk about powerless! Things can be challenging to understand and process when you're having to rely on others because you're not there to personally take care of things, and it's a totally different culture.

I had to keep looking at the prayer list I had made and put before God so that I could turn to Him in faith, knowing that He knew my heart, and that He would work all things for the good for everyone. It was such a challenge waiting and trusting others with one of the most important things in your life, your sibling, who, for the first time, couldn't speak for himself, and was in the most vulnerable position of his life. A fighter that he was most of his life because of who he was, now was lifeless, with no power left on this planet, and in the hands of strangers who may not have his best interests at heart, even at this time.

We were helpless here as well... only with a phone, trusting people in a different country. If it wasn't for the Holy Spirit's guidance and other siblings to bounce things off of, I don't know where I'd be. Then, there was the relief of people who suddenly felt free because they didn't have to deal with 'crazy' anymore. When I look at homeless people nowadays, I am so grateful that the Lord took him when He did, because who knows where he would be if the craziness hadn't stopped. He had wanted out of his misery since my father passed. That was really hard for him, and he talked about not wanting to be around anymore. He even wanted to take matters into his own hands. He didn't see his purpose here… he never saw it, and wondered why he was even here. I remember him telling my Dad that once he was gone, he wasn't going to be too far behind him and his words came true because not too long after, he wasn't.

I called him my King of Pain because that's all he knew how to experience in life, and if he wasn't in pain, he wasn't living. He didn't know what it was like to have a succession of joyful days. He was always up and down… mentally and emotionally. Maybe an earlier diagnosis and medication would have changed the situation, maybe not. We'll never know.

Do you ever feel that when you're on a roll, something happens that holds you back? Like you're constantly going two steps forward and three steps back? What's kept you from truly realizing your dream of being the person that's deep inside you? Is it people? Lack of confidence? Your upbringing? Things you can't put your finger on? Fear? It comes in different shapes and sizes. People are just as afraid of failing as they are of being successful.

They're afraid they don't have the skills to get there or that once they get there, they won't be able to sustain it once they're there. They will be like imposters living someone else's life. They will be found out and shamed.

Speaking of shame, when did yours start? For me, that word comes to mind when I think about my past and how I got here. I am ashamed of where I am. It started with the first 5 and it got worse with every pound that I gained after that. How could I have done so well and then wind up here, practically at the weight that I started?

Now, facing people that thought I was getting too thin was shameful because I felt like they'd think I'm a loser, that I couldn't sustain my new life, that I had failed, and they were right all along.

Shame rings throughout my life. I have to hide myself when I'm thin and hide myself when I'm fat. I hope it's OK to say that. I am fat. I'm very fat. I don't like that I'm fat, and I'm OK saying that about myself because at my weight and size, that statement is not too far out of range.

Shame, shame, the word is coming to mind, and it's not going away. This whole thing is shameful. Not dealing with things in life is shameful. What happened is shameful. Life has been shameful in one way or another. The shame I've felt through the eyes of others has caused me to want to hide under a rock and never come out. But alas, I am not one without hope in this world because that is what the Word is all about. Jesus died so I could always have hope and victory in every situation. So, I remind myself to cling to that because He has taken away my shame.

CHAPTER 15

The Zone

The ZONE... when you're in the zone, you can make and follow through on decisions like never before. There's a place your brain gets to where a switch is flipped, even if for a moment. A swift electric bolt that helps you put aside everything else and pursue this one thing. Getting yourself to that place is the biggest challenge because that is where the journey starts. It's that moment of clarity and resolve that jumpstarts your brain and your journey forward, giving you one little muster of strength that makes you believe you really can do this again.

In the zone, your mind is laser-focused on getting there and staying there. Mind mapping the plan to get you out is a breeze, and you're able to see the whole trip and how you're going to get to your destination, and nothing other than stopping for gas and going potty is going to deter you. You're determined to power through this and mow down anything that gets in your way. You're going to get it done, get it done now, and deal with whatever else is happening later.

Turning that switch on, though, can be more challenging for some than for others. You beat yourself up thinking you're a loser because everyone else seems to get it, and it just falls off them. You question why it has to be so hard for you. Why does it seem to come easily for others, while for you it's like climbing Mount Everest? You need a bunch of gear. You look at the whole picture, and it seems hard and seemingly impossible, so you choose to never start. The first step in any journey can be difficult, especially when you look back and realize you've got more failures behind you than you have victories.

Deep down, there's that little girl inside you who never fit in. She was always looked at differently by everyone. She was loved, but not in ways that made her feel valued and appreciated. It was in weird ways that I cannot even explain. Life was different for the little immigrant who didn't speak the language. I started out thin, until coming to the U.S., and not too long after, my personal weight battle started.

Things have to make sense to me. I like to get to the root of things... find ground zero, if you will. Although I'm not sure I will in this case. I tried going inside and figuring out if there was something that happened in the shadows that caused the surge in weight, which led to body shaming and wanting to hide from the world so that they wouldn't see me like this. I can't seem to pinpoint anything other than feeling horrible for the weight gain, not being accepted, and being bullied because I was different. My family was different; my parents were different. They spoke with an accent, and everyone thought they talked funny. I feel I've spent my life going up and down, and I'm still not sure why.

Once, when I was in my mid-forties, I embarked on this journey again for the umpteenth time. I was only 20-25 pounds away from my goal weight when I went for a physical and shared with my doctor that I wanted to get back to my mid-twenties weight. She then proceeded to tell me, "That's a pretty lofty goal for a woman your age." Imagine a young doctor, fresh out of medical school, telling that to one of her patients who wanted to get to a healthier weight. That stuck with me for a long time, and it's one of the voices I faintly hear every once in a while, when I get close to my goal weight. I push it back and remind myself of where she was in her life at the moment she made that statement. She had just had her first baby and was experiencing her own struggles with her weight and, most likely, was projecting that onto me.

As you now know, this isn't my first trip to the amusement park. I've been here many times in life with this same goal. So, my experiences each have their own little punk that tried to tell me that I couldn't do it. That I was getting too thin. It was them, in their own discomfort, and their issues, not mine. At times, my methods of getting where I was were a little unorthodox, but trust me, I never got "too thin." 😏 Don't let anyone tell you what your weight should be, or what a healthy one is, other than a good doctor. Not just any doctor, a good one. Someone who believes in proper nutrition, good health, and the whole person, not just the number on the scale.

As you may or may not know, there are many factors as to why people are where they are. It's not just because they had too many meals and didn't give a flip. The journey starts on the inside. Whether it's mental or internal. Get a thorough checkup. Have them check into your organs, blood, and family history. Sometimes the answer is there, and sometimes it's emotional. The good thing is that in the checking, the answers come.

CHAPTER 16

A Day In The Life Of Complacency

You know what it's like to live in the pandemic era. Most days are the same. You are in a fog, and you cannot seem to get yourself out. You see what is happening around you, and bewilderment is taking place within you. Every moment seems the same, and everything around you is just "there."

You're not sure what to do or what is the right thing to do at this particular moment. Should you move, should you stand still? Should you wait or should you keep moving? Do you reach out to others, or do you keep to yourself? Do you work, or do you sit around? Do you get creative, or does your mind shut down?

It's different for all of us. A couple of days may go by, and then you just can't take it anymore, and you have to do something... anything... just to get out of this rut.

It comes in spurts, and it's in moments. In some moments, you are stronger than others. Then the fog sets in, and you cannot see your way through anything other than being in a daze... drifting and just staring.

Drifting is the enemy's tool to keep us in a fog, complacent, and unfruitful. Without a vision, a focus, a desire that burns within you, these complacent days can just pile up. It's the accumulation, the impending new norm, which makes things difficult.

There are days in our lives when our frequencies will be a little higher than others. We are human, and stuff happens, and it's OK to have days to refuel, to be low key, and give our minds and bodies a rest. When it turns into mental fog and constant complacency drifting for too many days, that's when things start to get away from you. It's an accumulation of the days that make us feel crummy and want us to just dig deeper and bring the covers further over our heads.

How do we add things to our days to make them a little more productive, so we have mental engagement, something to hope for, to keep us from drifting into a rut? It's how we treat the days that bring on fogged complacency.

We examine ourselves and recognize when we are moving from the acceptable or high-frequency zone to the more challenging low-energy zone. Feel the difference when things are different, and your body is in need of rest or a regroup, so you can come back stronger, or when you are fighting with yourself because you know that you have something to do that is causing you to just drift, because there is an underlying reason why you're not doing that thing, and so now you're all over the place.

Do you know the difference between those? Do you have the strength, or do you know how to practice strength until it builds so you can move past those moments and bring yourself into a position of victory?

Do you know how to encourage yourself when you are low? Do you know how to take the complacency you're in and turn it into productivity, positivity, and forward movement towards your happy self? To create inertia so that you can get yourself to feel better?

I believe that a day lived in the life of a pandemic is like a day in the life of someone with the tendency to drift.

How do I keep myself from putting my mind in this mental prison? What is happening to me today? Great things have been happening, and I should be grateful and jumping for joy?

BIG decisions have to be made... things are uncertain, and deadlines are getting closer. I am choosing to close this day out positively... knowing that this will help someone else, and tomorrow will be better. The Lord is with me. He has not left me. More blessings are to come, and tomorrow is a new and beautiful day... a fresh start, and I get to recharge, regroup, and refocus on the wonderful life that the Lord has for me.

CHAPTER 17

A Voice For Annie

Annie couldn't and wouldn't talk because she was always listening to another voice that was speaking. It was the voice of doubt, fear, uncertainty, taunting, and unbelief. The voice that took away her confidence, challenged her faith, and stunted her life. It made her feel inadequate and unworthy of the things that were promised to her. It made her feel that she was not capable or worthy of a life of health, wealth, and overall success.

This voice talked in the morning, afternoon, and evening, sometimes encroaching on her dream life. The minute she woke up, the voice started, and it was a constant barrage of arrows throughout the day, to the point where the simplest of decisions could not be made. Every thought of getting out was challenged with a thought of 'you cannot, and I will have you here forever.'

It stole her life thought by thought, word by unspoken word. There was a veil on her mind, her eyes, and her ears. It was as if that veil was blocking the blessings that were attempting to come into her life. Occasionally, a little light would shine through that dark veil, but it was short-lived because the voice was always taunting her about the other shoe dropping and causing havoc.

There was always some type of accident, a ding, an unexpected thing happening. There was almost no escape except for the short reprieves of music and time with God. Even then, there was incessant knocking at the door to destroy the seeds and words deposited that would bring peace and life.

If there was any advancement at all, the voice would vehemently come in like a storm to attempt to take it away. To sweep and wipe its memory so it would not happen again. To take away the hope that one day, there would be a way out that would take her from this place and transport her to the Promised Land that was written in the Book.

Every attempt at moving forward, getting out, having goodness follow was destroyed by the voice. The voice also came through others. People constantly second-guessed her and did not want her to move forward. People who were jealous, unruly, and selfish. Children of the father of lies, born to do his bidding and used by him to oppress others. Sometimes, the sweetest of them, who had proven to be friends, were on assignment from the voice to steal, kill, and destroy that which she was trying to build.

They would come in like bullies with their words and their actions knocking down her sandcastle and laughing all the while. They took pleasure in it, in having the upper hand and making others feel less than what God created them to be. They fought at every turn, and nothing was good enough for them. No matter what you did for them, they always had something to complain about, a better way to do it, or a way they would have handled it that would have been better for you.

They aligned themselves with people that they thought would help them move forward just to get away from you, because you were so horrible and then, they themselves came crashing down in their own way, and the very thing that they said that they were getting away from, that you were supposedly unequipped to give them, or do for them, they ended up empty-handed and destroyed in the end.

"I'm getting out because it is taking too much time, and I want to take back my weekends," and then they get into something that takes all their time and their weekends. So ridiculous! They pretend to be your friends, but really, they are wolves in sheep's clothing.

One day, the Prince came. He showed Annie in His Word that this voice was a liar and the father of all the lies since the beginning of time.

One day, after hearing the Word over and over and letting it seep into her heart, she realized that her word mattered. Because of what He, the

Eternal Prince, had done for her, she had a voice. Her voice mattered. Because of His work, everything had to obey her voice. She was His and He was hers and that marriage was what made her have the power of attorney to change all things.

She realized how powerful and pertinent her voice was because just as the One in whom she was made in the image of, it had the capability to create life. The words she said were so important that nothing could stop her, and that was the precise reason why the voice kept her at bay and quiet. He was afraid that she would make a difference, that she would destroy his little rebellious and insignificant kingdom and would render him powerless to act in her life, quashing her impact in the lives of those around her.

He was more afraid of her than she should have ever been of him because he had been stripped of all of his power long ago. He could only roar, but not bite. Like any bully, he used scare tactics to make her think he had all the power, and she had none. That he was everything, and she was nothing.

Annie never felt like she had a voice in life. It always felt like people talked over her, through her, or around her. In recent days, especially today, she realized she did have a voice. That her words go out, and they don't come back void.

The Lord and the universe hear her. Her angels hear her. The objects around her hear her, and they have to obey her because that is what the Word says, and the Word is truth. So, little by little, Annie began to send her words out and with each victory she had, she used it as a memorial, treasuring it and keeping it as a memory that God was for her and not against her and although things would happen, they would not harm her in the way they were intended and that a life of peace was possible because the Son of God had come to set her free and bring her eternal life where she could spend her days in freedom, love, and worship.

Evening Thoughts...

YANA...You Are Not Alone.

MY JOURNAL PORTION

June 5, 2020

After several circumstances in life, my weight got out of control. I weighed more than I ever had before.

I got down a little bit by just starting somewhere and then continuing. I had asked the Holy Spirit for help because I didn't know what to do. I heard within me that I was eating the same as my husband, and I needed to eat half his portions. That's what got me started. I lost 35 pounds just by cutting portions. Then, I was at a stalemate for some time, and then cancer hit.

I was well for a while with no increase in weight. When the hysterectomy happened, my body and life changed even more. It seemed like all this stuff was happening around me and in me and there I was, left with all of these physical and hormonal changes. In my mind, I was determined that I was going to make some changes.

While trying to get on track and making progress to get back in full force, I was interrupted, and there was another setback, which caused me to seek more medical help, thus extending my healing time.

The interruption caused my bubble to deflate. I got so tired and totally unmotivated that I went back into my shell. It had been almost a year since a walk, or any sort of mobile activity had taken place. I was praying about something to do, some type of activity, or a device that would help me lose weight. I wanted to walk with my husband, but I couldn't walk outside during daylight. For us to walk together and avoid the sun and heat, it would have to be at 4:00 a.m.

I began praying to the Lord and giving Him my body in prayer because I just couldn't take all that was happening to it any longer. I had to leave it completely in His hands, as I had many times before, when there were no answers, and my emotions were everywhere.

It was Easter weekend, and I was watching TV. As I turned the channels, I came upon a commercial for the Total Gym. I was intrigued by people's results and thought it might help us. I stalled for a bit as I was mentally working out the logistics. I finally ordered ours because I couldn't get it, or the "only $1 to try it" out of my mind.

Starting out, the pain was intense! I was limited in the amount of time I had and the reps I could do. The pain I experienced afterwards from using muscles I hadn't used in a long time, along with the repurposing of my current body, was unbelievable!

I kept going, although sometimes it felt as if progress was so far off. At other times, I was amazed at how well I was doing, despite what had taken place in my body from the effects of breast cancer.

For months, the goal was to get back to some type of normalcy. There were days that were easier than others. In October, we decided to go on a modified eating plan to shed more weight. We started off with something we had intended to do years ago, and since using the new machine, a fresh incentive ignited within us, and we were finally both on the same page. Major prayer had been answered.

A couple of weeks in, we went out of town. Because this was a business trip for me, I was feeling extremely strict about staying on the plan. I wanted to wait until the event was over to exercise my "veering off" rights. He, on the other hand, was a little more lenient with himself. On our way home, during dinner, he shared something special that I wasn't aware of. I was excited by his sharing as it gave me hope and affirmed me. Although I was aware of his apprehension with the purchase, I prayed he would see the benefits.

He explained that although being a bit frustrated at first, as he was not really a gym type person, it came as a little more of a challenge to him than it seemed to be to me. However, after familiarity, repetition, and seeing his own results, it started becoming easier for him, and he was grateful for my purchasing it for us.

So when we arrived home, we dove into our journey. I was pleased that I had stuck with it for the 21 days before the trip, and that during it, I stayed true until a meal on the way home, where I allowed myself a baked potato with some butter and sour cream, along with a nice steak.

We went through the Holidays, our first one being Thanksgiving. I decided to make the same dishes we normally did, but with a healthier twist. So, each dish or item I was used to preparing now had a healthier alternative.

The green bean casserole was made from scratch with fresh beans, mushrooms, and my version of the soup, along with the traditional onion topping. The potatoes were Yukon Gold, which, unbeknownst to me at the time of purchase, were lower on the glycemic end.

The pies I made were fresh, down to the crust. The altered recipe of my favorite pie, double chocolate pecan, was so delicious. One of the ingredients for the recipe was honey, and the next day after I made it I realized I had not bought honey, I had gotten blue agave, which made the pie better for me with regard to sugar content and digestion. WOW... God is awesome, my mistake turned to my advantage!

We ate what we wanted the entire weekend: food, sweets, etc. I did not eat to the point of binging, but allowed myself the things I wanted to eat in good, healthy portions.

The last day of our "party," we pretty much finished everything. The next day, we went cold turkey, back to our prior eating plan. 😄 I weighed myself that morning. I had gained about 4 pounds, which I lost quickly over the next few days. We then continued until the Christmas Holiday and pretty much did the same thing with the New Year festivities.

Having our physicals in the middle of February, I found out that I had lost 30 pounds since my prior annual physical. I was so excited!!! We continued our journey, and then I was stuck at those 30 pounds for a while, only losing about a pound a week. As soon as I ate any type of carb, another pound was added, and it was very frustrating.

To get out of the rut, I tried another popular plan. Not sure I was doing it properly because I gained about 4 pounds in a couple of days. After I had purchased all the food for it, I realized that the diet I really wanted to do was Scarsdale, as I had done it in my junior year of high school and had great success. After a couple of days on that high-fat diet, we switched.

Two weeks… ugh, it wasn't easy, but the weight was coming off at almost a pound a day, which made it easier to keep going. I was tired and depleted, but continued with my exercise program and the eating plan. After the two weeks were up, the total weight loss was about 10 pounds. I've managed to keep it off for a couple of weeks, and now I'm at another plateau.

June 7, 2020

Today I'm tired. Yesterday was so busy, and my food intake was a little different. I had some carbs, and it was good to veer off a little bit. Nothing major, but because of how we've been eating, it seemed major. Less than the craziness of the prior weekend though.

This whole week, I've increased my cardio a little each day to offset last weekend. I am now in a *bit of a holding pattern, in a good way. I feel that I've been able to take a breath and figure out what plan I want to use next. It feels good that I can veer off a little and still stay below where I want to be as far as a set point.*

This coming week, I will be looking into which plan will be the next adventure. My goal is to lose about 10 pounds in the next 6 weeks, as we have a family event coming up.

I want to be able to attend at a different weight. Even though I'm already at a lower weight and very close to my goal, it's not where I ultimately want to be, especially for an event where I haven't seen family for a long time.

I want to make a statement. I am taking care of myself. I have been able to reach a crazy goal in my mid-50s, after some serious life challenges, illnesses, and surgeries. As everyone else has been gaining throughout the years, I have been able to turn this around. Not in my own strength, because I know the Lord is strengthening me, and I want this win for all the changes that have taken place in this little body.

A couple of years ago, I saw a before-and-after picture of a well-known and beloved mentor in my field. When I saw the picture of her transformation, it was very encouraging to me as I knew she had some life challenges herself. It was hormonally based because of age and menopause, but encouraging just the same.

I would not be taking anything medically to offset what was happening to me, just like I opted out when I had cancer and they wanted me to take some crazy medication for the rest of my life. I needed my changes to come from a food and exercise aspect, a more comfortable way that has brought many wins to my life.

I had a new resolve within me. I learned to bring my concerns before God first. Even when I was at a whiny stage, He was good at listening. In doing that, I gained peace, perspective, and strength. I saw over and over how putting my biggest concerns at His feet helped me to come from a peaceful, strategic place that I couldn't think of on my own, or when my mind was not in a good state to fully think things through.

I'd like to say I lost weight and stayed there, but that has not been my life. However, I am looking towards my future, and the picture I see in my mind is what I want my story to be. Despite major life interruptions, I am continuing, no matter how long it takes to get there.

I think that it is a very doable thing, even at this stage in my life. I want my hope to increase and to give hope to others around me. No matter what you've been through in life, you can take control of it and design your future, not just in this aspect, but in all aspects of your life.

A vision is the most important thing needed to make anything come to pass in life. Whatever area you are working on, without a vision, it will not happen. It has been proven time and again throughout history. Whether it's family, spirituality, career, weight, or finances, you can reboot and change what you're seeing and create something different.

You have to see yourself in a different place in your mind before it will fully materialize in your life. I have had this happen to me so many times, in both positive and negative aspects, in all areas of my life. I have seen it in my health, my relationships, my career, my finances, my body, and weight.

June 15, 2020

I have stepped backwards in the process. The past couple of weeks, I have experienced a stalemate. We have not had a plan that we're following. We are just taking a break from the goal of watching everything, including the scale going down. This was such an intense focus for a while, and then it had to be put aside so we could regroup, reassess, and reaffirm the WHY, so we could keep going in the best way for us.

Although we have been eating a little off course, there have been a few things we haven't been willing to go back to. There is still a point of no return to the old lifestyle. We have been exploring other options, but nothing to the extreme of where we were before. Which I guess is something to be proud of.

There are some functions coming up, that I want to be "fit" for. I do not know what it is about revealing a new me to myself that is so appealing. It's like a show of great restraint and a statement that says, yes, you can reclaim your body at any age, and no matter what you've gone through. I guess that is the statement… that despite it all, we've been able to reach this goal.

I am trying not to see myself as a failure during this pandemic thing. I was feeling great and powerful until I started veering off and now gaining just over 5 pounds, wiping out almost a month's worth of work! So, now I want to take drastic measures to get that off quickly to get back on track, like I'm making up for lost time.

So… what is next for me? I think I'm going to purge, like I've been used to most of my life. It's a pattern that has been part of me forever, but this is different because the emotion is not ruling my life like it did in the past. I remember well the emotional downtroddenness that I've experienced.

It's been a really stressful time. It feels like the whole world has gone crazy. At first, it was OK because it was a virus. Although people were panicking around us, I felt OK inside. Despite the darkness and uncertainty around me, I prayed for everyone, encouraged them, and was grateful for the little silver linings before me. Through helping others and looking for every little bit of the Light of God, I could see that this situation was the best way for me to cope with what was going on.

June 21, 2020

On Friday, the pain in my brain was so bad. The thoughts that were racing through my mind were unbelievable. The uncertainty, the thoughts of losing, of hopelessness for the situation, the dates that were coming up, the deadlines that may not be met in most areas of life, not just in body, and it was coming at me like a ton of bricks.

For the past two weeks, I've been adding 15 extra minutes a day, about 5 miles more on the bike, which I thought would help the situation, and I'm still climbing, but then again, where would I be if not for these extra miles and time? Would I have gained more?

Anyway, an alert came through from a ministry I like for a new video they put up. This was posted on Friday afternoon, and I didn't listen to it until Saturday morning's workout. It was all about oppression and how the enemy is using it during this time to make people feel hopeless.

I believe this oppression is a factor in my going backwards. I just wanted to say, "What the heck, it's only one meal or just a little treat," and keep going. Now that this looming event is right around the corner, I don't want to let myself down.

The thing is that in the past we kept going, taking things into consideration (wedding, Holidays, etc.), staying off for just the one day, the one event, and then going right back on track.

Also, now we are at a different set point. We haven't been at this set point in a while, and maybe that has something to do with things. It's a great place to be, and it is to be applauded. At the same time, though, we should not be resting on our laurels.

I would love to just work virtually with the occasional get together for appointments. Am I crazy to like this virtual world so much? I enjoy being behind the screen and keyboard, and just work from there. Flashback to my first big corporate job. WOW! I remembered back to how I used to love to type letters on the Word Processor.

Have all the things I've experienced brought me to this place? Maybe people will think I'm nuts. Is it wrong to just want a residual income, where you're doing something that brings peace and harmony to others, brings in what you need, and helps you and others live life to its fullest?

I had wanted certain things in my life, and then I'm not sure where, but it all went somewhere I had not expected. With each little decision and thing that happened, my life changed. It became something I never dreamed of. It became what I had not thought or expected.

I thought I would be married early, have children early, rear them, live in New England in a nice home, maybe have a beach home we could all retreat to, and come together on

Holidays and special days. To celebrate the seasons, my favorite Holidays commencing and ending the Summer. Memorial Day, 4th of July, Labor Day, enjoying the ocean and the wonderful bustle of these Summer Holidays. To have my children and their children gather with me.

That has not happened. Neither with my personal life, or business, at least in my eyes. I thought I would be in a certain place in business by now, having put my time in, and having it reward me financially, and with people in my life that I had shared the journey with. The diversions and distractions are both amazing and unbelievable!

Now wanting to make these changes, I started wondering if I was just now waking up to this new thing, or was everything just a setup for this specific time? Was I supposed to be a sharer, blogger all along, and this is the time for it to be taking place now? For such a time as this, like Esther?

All my life, I've been a professional visitor. I have shared the lives of others, helping them through their darkest moments, not living the life I wanted or dreamed of. Every once in a while, there is a burst of freshness, something new that gives me strength to believe and move to the next level, and then, I fall back into patterns I don't like through some event or my own mind.

I feel like I'm typing away like a moron with no real life or future. I feel like David the Psalmist. One minute I'm up, and one minute I'm down. One minute, the Word has me fired up, and the next minute, I can't figure out how I can make my life something of worth or value to society. It's as if being in this place of undauntedness will keep me in Lodebar (a Biblical place of low living literally and figuratively) forever. Not the truth, though. Things can change, and things can and have been getting better.

Financially, if I were to measure myself, at this age and time in my life, I am certainly not where I want to be. I know there are others in this world who would want to switch places with me, but for myself, I feel I'm living below where the Lord would expect one of His children to live.

I've been writing for the longest time today... getting all this stuff out, hoping it will change something inside me and around me, and if it ever gets out, either in a book or a blog, that it will help someone.

I am here to help the hopeless get some hope. To let them know that it's never too late in life to want to make a change and rewrite a story.

Where am I now? I am married to a man I love who loves me. Not all things are perfect. I am not perfect. I have not had any children. I do not live in the house I've always wanted, and I do not have a beach home I can retreat to. I do not have a successful business full of people I've shared goals and memories with, that have led us all to a place of abundance, spiritually or financially. I do not have a big nest egg waiting for me, a path carved out for security for people at our age. I feel like I'm just here. That's it!

Where to now? What changes need to be implemented so that significant transformation can take place to catapult me to a new place in life? Something that will restore the years the Lord has given me, to make all the craziness worth something. To come out of the furnace without smelling of smoke.

At the beginning of this virus, I took great joy in preparing meals and documenting them, and now, with everything happening, I have retreated somewhat. I want that back. I feel that I could do more of this. This type of work seems easier, creatively entertaining, and there is a more pleasing fulfillment. Easier to plant seeds and water them to influence life and growth.

I know that there will be rejection in a way, like other areas in life. There are people who will like you or not. Who will follow you or not. Who will agree with you or not. I've seen the comments online and from followers on other platforms. Some people can be pretty brutal, or a source of encouragement to forge forward.

You can't really argue with someone's specific story. The way they see things or what they've been through. It's their story, and somehow, that gives me some comfort. It's my story. Whether you agree with what I've done or haven't done. Where I am at this point in life, based on what *you've accomplished in yours, is your life, not mine.*

All I can do, and I think this is what God expects from all of us, is that we live ours for an audience of One, and encourage others to live theirs. If there is something we can each glean from our existence here that can help others navigate more efficiently and with less pain, then we've made progress.

It's all about living better. Living the Scriptures so we can all live more abundant lives. I think, based on the Words of our Lord, and how I see others live those words out, that He came for our victory, our abundance, and our smiting the things that the enemy throws our way, towards the pursuit of this victorious life. John 10:10 promises us that. That is one Scripture that I want to stand on. In my most uncertain times, I don't even know what to call it… my most mentally powerful times, when I thought that I deserved certain things because of the victory God wanted us to have, I ended up overcoming and getting the things my heart was set on. That is how I see this. God, giving me power, through faith, to be able to overcome the fiery darts that have been thrown at me.

June 25, 2020

It's a beautiful day and I have some newfound energy. I want to declutter, within me and without. My inner and outer house. How to organize your house? One room and one thing at a time. Staying in the room, or with that one thing until it's finished, is important. It's when I go from one room or thing to another that it takes a little longer.

Make a list of the things you'd like to accomplish because, without a list, it's so easy to get distracted. Sometimes the distraction happens even with the list. However, the list helps you see what needs to be done and will keep you on track without getting distracted by other potential projects you see throughout the house. You can snap out of your drifting by looking back at your notes. Like reading a book and finding the last sentence you read, so you can keep reading from there.

Also, give yourself a time frame. I like to be in contests, and this is just another challenge with myself. Equally important is the one-touch method. Picking things up and doing what you need to do with them helps cut down on time, because handling the same thing multiple times, moving it from one place to another, not knowing what to do with it, is a huge time waster.

The same goes for mail. We get so much junk mail it's a wonder we still have trees. How did these companies get the right to send us this junk? It's amazing! Having been in marketing and sales, I know it's important, but I still find it annoying as it takes time to sift through. There are websites that you can go to and sign up so you do not receive unwanted mail. Unsubscribe, like back in the day when you could get on a "do not call list" for telemarketers.

Do you like to work out and yet, every morning it's the same story... I don't want to get out of bed, I'm tired, I have to get my stuff together. Whatever your specific story is that you tell yourself so you don't have to work out, you can remedy and eliminate those emotions by preparing the night before. For those who work out at home, like me, it's easy to get up and get ready. I think if I had to drive somewhere, that would be a bit of a deal breaker.

Being very cognizant of my time and wanting to shower before I'm out and about, I like to work out at home. So, exercise for me has to be the first thing. There are many reasons I prefer the home workout. It's a guaranteed sanitary environment. I have my privacy and the machines to myself. Not to mention the beautiful quietness it affords me. Last but most certainly not least, I don't feel like driving 30-40 minutes to get to a gym to do my workout. By the time I drive back and forth from the session, I could be done with my workout, shower, and on to my next thing. There were times when I've gone to gyms, and I like getting to know people and working out in groups, but at this stage in life, I prefer to do it at home and on my own.

I like getting up before the rest of the world is up. Everything I need to start my workout has been prepared ahead of time, so there is no question *in my mind of my next steps, or making excuses not to workout. I just get in there and do it. Sometimes, thinking about getting those things together can potentially give me reason to skip the workout. It also saves me about 15 minutes or more by being prepared, not to mention the mental back and forth I'll do in my mind with what to wear, and where it is.*

I get it together, and I jump in. I don't check anything that is coming at me when I turn on my device. I go straight to what I am going to listen to while I'm exercising, so there aren't any distractions. This is also my time with the Lord. I listen to positive messages that teach me the Word so I can be victorious in life.

Next, do a great workout. Just do your best. Sometimes, when I'm feeling low on energy, I will put on some jamming tunes that I have put in a playlist for myself that will get me going. I have several playlists based on my mental state that day and what I want to accomplish. Even to the point of loudness in my ears so that it knocks out the voices inside that are keeping me from getting into the groove I need to have for a great workout.

I also encourage myself. I remind myself that it's only "x" number of minutes out of my day, so I give it my all because it's only a short period of time in comparison to my whole day. I can do this for one hour, let's say, or I can do this for two more reps. I just keep coaching myself to the next step.

It's so peacefully quiet outside; sometimes it's still dark, but this time is precious to me. It's a big excitement that gets me up in the morning. Having done this makes me feel so accomplished. Getting the workout in, my message in, my shower in, I am feeling great. It's like all is well with the world, and I'm set for my day. No matter what comes at me, at least I've done these things before the rest of the world around me has even gotten up for coffee.

July 4, 2020

Turning point...

Out of nowhere, things happen that throw us for a loop and disrupt our lives. Other people's carelessness and distractions end up affecting us.

I couldn't believe it. What the heck was happening? I know it's spiritual because just the night before, I was on a call with friends and I was testifying to His goodness, praising Him for all the wonderful things He'd done in and with my life. I was being blessed so much, and then this.

I had even had a chat with my brother, and I felt like the Lord had been showing me things through our conversation. Curses being broken, changes being made. I am asking the Holy Spirit to help me remember this call, where I reached out to give him early birthday wishes.

I tried my best to stay focused on other things in my life and stay on track with what I had started, and it just became harder, but the stress of things just got to me somehow.

I got down in weight to almost out of the 40's. I think one day I actually saw 139 on one of the scales, and then there was a turn! We started eating a meal here and there, got off track, and now, here I am, 10 pounds later.

So, after a few weeks of just doing whatever without a plan with regards to food, there's been an accumulation of about 10 pounds. I just kept indulging on little things until now.

Things have been stressful. I've been craving sugar and wondering where these intense cravings are coming from. Maybe my body is still in PMS mode. I thought maybe my body was still thinking it's that time of the month. It could be that the whole stress of this time is just piling up. I thought I had it under control. There are several factors that may be contributing.

Maybe self-sabotage because I'm so close to the goal. I mean, God forbid I reach it. Like other areas, it feels the same. All the work being done, and then right before you're there, it happens, you lose it, and you're behind.

Then there were the thoughts of "Who do you think you are?" God doesn't want to bless you. You must go through stuff just like everyone else. Some say this Christian life is all about suffering, and unless we're suffering, we're not living. Well, I was remarkably familiar with that, and I didn't want to be.

It was a busy and exhausting day as we somehow attempted to celebrate Independence Day. I had a burger for dinner; it was really good, with blue cheese and tomato... so good.

July 5, 2020

Last night, I kept waking up almost every half hour. I just couldn't get myself to sleep through. I woke up a few times to pee and at 3:30 a.m. I was wide awake. I was having the strangest dreams. They've been very vivid for the past few days. I prayed to be able to go back to sleep instead of starting the day with a workout at this hour and then sleeping after a shower.

Yay! Got back to sleep and woke up at 6:00 a.m. and worked out. It was a good one! Thank you, Jesus. Then more treats... not happy about it, ready to move on.

I'm looking forward to getting back on track tomorrow. I want to get that determination again... get in the zone so that I can get to the goal. I want to see that 139 again and get lower.

We have a wedding coming up at the beginning of August. I'm wondering if they will still be able to have it with the resurgence of the virus. Regardless, we are starting back up on Monday.

Tomorrow I will be tapering down to get ready for Monday. It will be the two-week plan again. I'm looking forward to it and am praying for the strength to continue with it and keep going from there to reach the goal of 120.

I want to reach the goal quickly. I believe that since I have built a new setpoint, it will be easier this time. I am grateful to have been able to go from my highest weight of 205 to where I am now. Despite the recent increase, it's still a 55-65-pound loss. I have to be excited about that and be grateful for it, even if I've put on a couple and I'm not overly thrilled with where I am now.

July 6, 2020

Happy Birthday Joey, I love you!!!! 🫧

This morning I heard several things that really hit me. I love the wee hours of the morning, listening to your Word, to the silence around me, and that peace that comes with it before anyone is up and about.

I feel that as long as I'm in this state, the enemy of my soul thinks he can keep me quiet, and I won't say anything in faith, and will not be able to have an impact. That hit me because when I try to speak up, he tries to challenge me through calamity so there will be a loss, and I will clam up as I take up the distraction of fixing things, or look at what's happening and hear that I don't have the faith to believe, declare, and receive.

I think this has been a pattern my whole life, and I want to break that pattern. WOW... maybe I am predictable? That's what's been happening. Move forward a little, and I will keep you back somehow.

Newsflash… you are the loser. You are the one who is going to live eternity in hell with no way out, not me. Genesis says I am made in His image; you are not. I am given all that He has for me, and no one can take that away. All the promises that are in His Word are available to me, and they cannot be taken from me. I am claiming them and will continue until they all come to pass.

Getting lots of flashes from my past today… hasn't happened like that in a while… maybe it's all the sugar and junk I've been ingesting.

July 12, 2020

Psalm 103, My benefit package.

Salvation means wholeness. Something with no pieces missing. If there is something missing, then we are not whole. God wants us to be all set spiritually, physically, emotionally, relationally, and financially.

If one of those areas is lacking, then we are not whole. It's not OK to settle for one area not being fulfilled. The weapon can be formed, but it doesn't have to prosper.

This pandemic weapon has been formed, but it is not going to prosper in my life. I am believing that despite what is happening around me, Psalm 91 is in place in my life. I am dwelling in the secret place of the Most High, under the shadow of the Almighty, and I am saying of HIM... HE is my refuge and my fortress, HE is my God, and I trust HIM. HE will make all things work together for good for me and for James.

Am I being selfish, sticking my head in the sand, or maybe it looks like I do not care about what is happening around me? NOPE, today I am being firm in exercising my Kingdom Covenant I have with the Lord. Though a thousand fall at my side, and ten thousand at my right hand, it will not come near me.

Affirmation and prayer...

HE has given HIS angels charge over me so that I do not even gash my foot up against a stone.

HE says that I can declare a thing and it will come to pass. That by my words, I am either acquitted (justified) or condemned, and I am not going to use my own mouth to create a life that I do not want. I am going to be free, abiding in a house I adore, that has been made just for me, and living the life of my dreams.

The only way I know to make that happen is through my faith. Faith that what the Word of God says is the truth, and that truth will set me free. I am going to be at my goal weight. I will have my needs met, I will prosper and be in good health... my soul is prospering, and that will make all other things come to pass.

July 20, 2020

Allow the Holy Spirit to paint a picture of a glorious future on your soul.

2 Corinthians 4:4 satan blinds the mind of people, don't let him blind you to your inheritance!

July 25, 2020

Got some stuff done around the house today and got some meal plans typed up. Still weird from the past couple of days of eating.

Recovering from the other night's faux pax. I cannot believe it! Both of us. I feel like I wasted God's money. I didn't want to make a scene, but I will never go back to that place. I cannot believe how people can serve food like that. It's just amazing to me. I want to get better at cooking and seasoning myself so we can be more precise and not feel like we just consumed an entire saltshaker in one sitting or with one meal.

I'm also tired from work. Yesterday was an exhausting day. I didn't get to have lunch. I was feeling it this morning and I've been kind of off today. I am praying to be more energetic tomorrow.

THANK YOU for being with me the past few days and helping me do some great workouts. I so appreciate the energy you give me to do that, and for the healing that has already taken place in my body.

Today, I was reminded of my authority as I was listening to music. I wish I could remember what sparked it. I had a thought and said no you don't... maybe it was associated with a song.

August 16, 2020

A couple of weeks ago, we decided to start something rolling. A conversation came up that others were waiting, and maybe we should too. I said that they were not like we were. We believed differently, and sowed differently and therefore we should expect different results.

Yesterday we watched The Grapes of Wrath, and with everything that was going on in the world at that time, a story was being told by one man who had gone to California to those who hadn't gone there yet. He told his story, but then the main character responded with "Whose dream is it?" Like that wasn't his dream, and he was not going to listen to the failure that happened to him. He was going to make his own dream, and that was going to be what happened to him. Not all the craziness and negativity that the man was describing to him.

So, I looked at James and said, "This is our dream. Our dream is different than what our friends are doing. Our dream is not the same as theirs, and we don't believe the same. That is why we are doing what we're doing, and not doing it the same as others." It reminded me of what I had said a few weeks ago.

Like a confirmation to continue in the dream that was in our hearts. Thank you, Lord!!!

August 22, 2020

Went out for dinner tonight and used the gift certificate we were given. It was interesting. The news says few people are out because of the pandemic, but all the places we drove by were full, with lines waiting to enter.

Curbside pickups were busy as well as the drive-thrus. Our server said she had been making less money since they opened up after the pandemic than before. It made me wonder if people were just going out, spending money on meals they couldn't really afford, and not caring about the staff and their tips.

The meal was OK. We got served after two big parties that came after us, and although our steaks were cooked well, our food was not hot.

We stopped at the Cheesecake Factory, got dessert and coffee, came home afterwards, got into our PJs, and enjoyed them with a movie. All in all, it was a great night, and I am grateful to have had the opportunity to be out.

Our server was telling a story about her going to school and her family, and I gave her a pretty big tip. It was more than our meal now that I think about it. It was great to be a blessing!

Afterwards, I was checking some things online, and because the seminar which I paid for was botched up due to internet issues, we are going to be refunded our fee, which is amazing because it was the amount of the tip I left at the restaurant. I thought of a recent sermon about the different types of giving and the returns of *the Lord. I saw it working in my life with my own two eyes! Thank you, Lord!*

August 23, 2020

This morning was a little rough. I haven't had a potato or treats in a while, and we even ate the popcorn I got in my seminar packet.

Needless to say, the night was a little rough with the salt, sugar, and stuff.

It was all I could do to down my tea, workout, and get last night's meal out of my system. It felt so good to shower and get the salt out of me. Then I had some fruit, and afterwards we relaxed a little before taking on the tasks I'd written for myself. Despite how icky I felt from my food intake, I was able to get everything on my list done. I'm not happy about all I consumed, but I will make the best of it today by making healthier choices and scaling down a bit to give my body a little break so it can process yesterday.

September 27, 2020

It's ALL about YOU….

You know "those" people. They can play a big part in your life or a small part, but they are there. Maybe you have one, or multiples and no matter what is happening to you, it's always all about them.

You can go out, share a great meal, but the conversation is about them. Your heart may be broken into pieces, you are bleeding on the inside, and they are oblivious to your pain, your distance, your tone, and your whole situation. Even though they may be so close to you that they know exactly what's going on, no matter where the conversation turns, it still circles back to them.

Then there are the ones who always have something going on in life. Somehow, they cannot seem to get ahead. There is always a little tragedy that keeps them down. They are consistently moving two steps forward and three steps back, and they can't find their way out of a paper bag despite the encouragement and help from all areas of life. Somehow though, it's your fault, because you're moving on and attempting to live your best life, and on your way or close to your finish line.

They feel that since you seem to have it together and seem to not have any problems, not because you don't have any, but you're good at managing them and keeping them lower key. Meanwhile, they are screaming the whole way about every little thing that happens in their life, and so they keep talking, because they think you don't have anything to talk about.

Be protective of your sphere. Live in your bubble, swim in your lane, so to speak. Have protection around you so that you are not affected by these energy drainers. Keep living with your armor on so you don't get pierced. Be like the Michelin Man. Some people gain weight to protect themselves from being hurt... that is another story.

Recognize what is happening and protect your sphere, your world. Many experts have touched on watching your 5, those 5 people around you. To guard the influencers in your life. Those you share your time, life, dreams, success, and hiccups with.

Sometimes dreams are so precious that they must be written down and guarded until they come to pass. Every step has to be hidden until the dream is a reality. Then, you will have safely reached your destination with fewer obstacles and roadblocks along your path, and the undeniable results will be seen by all.

The words of others can sometimes keep us from the things we most want and need. When we're forced over time to be quiet and stay in the shadows for so long that we do not have a voice, or want to have one, it robs us of a fulfilling life.

There is a balance to it all. Learning to live quietly in the shadows, having fulfilling relationships, and living the life of your dreams.

How? Guard yourself in vulnerable times when an idea is hatching.

Understand the lives of those around you, and if the air starts to get toxic, find some oxygen fast.

Put that mask on and breathe it in so you don't lose consciousness.

Let your light shine, even if people don't see or refuse to recognize who you really are. Even Jesus was not recognized as a prophet in His own town. What does that mean? Sometimes people are so familiar with you that they see you just one way and refuse to see the potential within you.

Sometimes, as sad as it may be, you may just have to walk away and let them find someone else to cry to and poop on so that your life can be saved.

I think I used to be one of those people. There was so much going on in my life, and things around me were just nuts. I didn't know how to live a normal life with the way I grew up... it wasn't horrible, just different.

Things weren't the same as what was going on around me. Because of our culture, we were the oddballs. I always felt like I stuck out like a sore thumb. I was between two worlds... one foot in one, and one foot in the other... like there were two me's. The me that was the daughter of immigrants trying to keep our heritage alive, and the other me who was trying to be like the rest of the kids and families I went to school with. Wanting to have their lives and not have so much overprotectiveness and craziness. I wanted to be normal. At the time, normal seemed to be outside my house, not in it. Now I look back, and wonder if the walls in our home were the normal ones, and what was beyond the front door was the crazy.

I felt like such a fish out of water for so long that it feels like it took forever to get to where I am today. I always looked at others as normal and myself as abnormal. Why is that? I was always trying to fit into someone else's idea of life.

Whose mold are you trying to fit into? Are you so distracted by what's going on around you that you don't see the beauty and the wonder that you were created to be? Are you trying to conform and fit into the 'jeans' that were given to you by someone who has no clue who you are... wearing them, whether you are going to *turn blue and have no circulation, because you want to feel accepted and to fit in?*

This has been my life story in so many areas. Career, relationships, and weight. Everyone else's life seemed so much more interesting than mine that I forgot how to live my own life as an individual with things that mattered to me, and not just what mattered to everyone else.

I was an imposter living someone else's life, instead of finding out who I was, what I wanted, and who I wanted to be. I got into things that I wanted to do and then continued long after it was time to go... like staying too long at a party... overstaying your welcome. When things didn't work out the way I thought, I would blame myself and go into a slump.

What did I think was so horrible about me that I had to be someone else? Afraid to stand up to my own beliefs and standards. Maybe it stemmed from when I was younger, and I carried it through the rest of my life. Was I in the background or on the sidelines so long that I had no idea how to live? A trophy sometimes, or something to have, but not to hold. Temporary stuff, nothing stuck.

So… all these years later, I am taking this time to figure out who I am. Who I want to be. To recapture and take back the things I want and to develop the things that are inside me that I have stuffed deep down. Those things I was afraid to develop. Like writing… putting my feelings down because no one wanted to hear them or was interested in them.

I didn't want people to end up like me… with all the struggles I went through. If I could prevent someone from wasting time, energy, or life so that they can climb the mountain faster or easier, point them to a shorter and more fruitful route, that is what I'd like to do.

Why make some mistakes if you can see what others have done and learn from them as much as you can? Making your own mistakes and learning from them is sometimes overrated. You can still learn just as much from others as if you made the mistake for yourself.

Don't sell yourself short and think that you have to experience all sorts of grief and trouble so you can have a learning experience that helps you grow into who you're supposed to be. Not everyone has to go to the school of hard knocks.

The weird thing is that I am waiting for the day to end so that I can go to sleep, so I can work out tomorrow and weigh myself. I'll get to see how much I've lost, and see if I've reached a new pinnacle that I haven't been to in decades.

Isn't that strange... I am trying to recapture something, an experience that I had years ago, a feeling of when I was young and in control of my life. A time when I felt great about myself, was free, loved life, and was in some kind of control. New things were happening. I was on my own. I was in charge of my decisions and the plans I made for myself. I was on the brink of trying new things, renewing my life, bettering myself, and seeking new opportunities to live the life I always dreamed of.

I thought school was the thing, a new home that I could turn into an investment, a new life away from those things that I felt were holding me back. I was advancing and doing things that were helping me advance. Things I'd never done before, and for the first time in my life, I was proud of myself and who I'd become. Then who did I become after that? It's almost like I got to a certain place, then I got scared and shrank back. I was afraid I couldn't continue in that success and fulfill the dream all the way through. I didn't think I had the strength to go to the end of the road, and those around me made sure I didn't through their extreme cautiousness and lack of encouragement.

September 30, 2020

I am going to do something BIG just like my Dad said. I'm not sure how it will come about, but I will!! The Holy Spirit, my Counselor, will show me things to come and guide me into all truth. My words will make me millions!

Don't make any major decisions until you go up and come back. Like Moses, go up the mountain and come back with His plan.

Self-care... your face, your heart, your ears, your mind, your body...

Your face... what are you doing to take care of the first thing that people see when they look at you? Are you giving it proper self-care? Are you cleansing and washing away the accumulation of the day? Are you moisturizing to iron out the kinks that were caused by what you experienced that may have put some stress on your skin?

Your heart... are you guarding your heart right now? Keeping it healthy and staying peaceful? In a time like this, when there is so much going on around us, it's more important than ever to guard our hearts with all diligence. Create a barrier between you and the news of what is going on. Be hopeful that all will work out for you and not against you. Believe that life happens for you and not to you.

Your heart is one of the lifelines of your body. It needs to be steady and at peace, unless it's working out and required to beat faster. Unhealthy pumping will cause it to be taxed.

Make sure that whatever is causing an unhealthy beat gets beat out of your life. 😄

Your ears... what are you listening to? Are you hearing things that lift you up or tear you down? Are words of fear, lack, division, distress, or hopelessness in earshot? Or are you in a safe place, hearing love, peace, and kindness? What you hear permeates your body, your soul, and then it starts to form your thoughts, and your thoughts form what you do next and who you become. Guard what you let into those two portholes that are in between that special part of your body... your brain.

Your brain... mind... how are you treating it... how are you managing it? Are you guarding the thoughts that are coming into it? Are you guarding it so it stays healthy and free to serve you? Are you letting good and wholesome thoughts in, canceling out the pummeling ones, so that they do not permeate and cause you to think and do things you would not normally do? Are you guarding how you think? Because how you think affects your whole body. Your thoughts can provide peace, energy, and health.

Watch the thoughts, think on the good ones, and discard the ones that are bringing distress and tripping up your system, causing you to halt, panic, be helpless, and stuck.

Your body... what are you doing to help the beautiful thing that God created to last longer and be healthy in that process? Are you feeding it and watering it like a precious plant? Are you giving it the sunshine it craves? Are you giving it the sleep it needs? Are you exercising it so that your organs and endorphins are healthy?

A good exercise program should give you peace, energy, and should feel good for your body when you're done. Yes, some workouts are a little more taxing than others. Sometimes we have to work a little harder to reach a goal or to get more out of it, but at least you're doing something... do something to get your body going, and give it the love it deserves.

My desire is for you and me to come out better after this is over than how we went in. To gather what we can while we are in this, so what we take out will have a positive impact on how we live and manage life. A reset to how we do things and handle things. Taking what we've learned and using it on a daily basis to get through life easily and have seamless future transitions.

God has an image of you, and so does the enemy. The reason he's coming so fiercely for you is because he sees God's favor on you.

He sees the image of strength inside you that he has been trying to quash your entire life. The image that you get of yourself after you've been attacked is not the image of God, it's the image that the enemy wants you to have.

That's why he attacks you! To bring you down. To bring you low to the image that he wants you to be, not the image that God sees of you.

If he did not see the image of God within you, he would not try to pull you down or try to mold you into the image that he wants you to be. The image he has for you, the image of defeat, failure, and desolation, is the image of all that he is, because he chooses not to worship God. The image of him falling down into the abyss.

The image of him burning in the Lake of Fire for all eternity!

Verse of the Day...

1 Peter 1:3 "Blessed be the God and Father of our Lord Jesus Christ, who according to His abundant mercy has begotten us again to a living hope through the resurrection of Jesus Christ from the dead." (KJV)

October 1, 2020

Will it always be like this? Not necessarily. Sometimes you have to do extreme things to cross over the goal. Once the goal is reached, you can relax a little and move into maintenance mode. However, that mode does not mean that you get to pick up your old habits and continue in them, because then you will be back to where you were before you started.

Maintenance means you are now managing and upholding the current level you've reached. Not at the old level and still living the same way because then maintenance will no longer be called maintenance… it will be a reversion.

Perception…

I always looked around at other people. I wondered what they did, how they did it, what their thoughts were that led them to do what they did. How much money they made, how they handled it. What types of houses they lived in, what they drove.

Mainly, it was how they produced and what caused them to produce in such a fruitful manner.

Not realizing that within myself, I had a manner of production. I could walk into a room and see what was wrong with the situation, see what needed attention, what needed to be straightened out, or to fill the lack that was in it.

So why was I looking at others? Why was I watching them, thinking so little of myself?

Is it a character trait? A habit I formed without recognizing it until it got big? Was it something

I learned from one of my parents, or those I was close to when I was growing up?

Where did this come from? Is it the monster of comparison?

Even in business, I always looked at others as if they had something that I would never have. I looked at them as smarter than me and more productive than me, like they had a magic formula or something special that got them to where they were that I would never possess.

Even when I reached pinnacles of what others had not reached, having it done legitimately, I still felt like an imposter and like I should not be there, and someone was going to find me out and bring me down.

Imposter syndrome… like you're living someone else's life and you're going to be exposed.

When we moved here, I looked around and wondered how these people lived behind closed doors. I don't know why, but I thought others' lives were more interesting and important.

October 3, 2020

It's that time of year again. October, the month attributed to breast cancer, mammograms, and all things to do with that. It's a tender time of year for me. It was in this month that I was diagnosed, which started my special journey.

I never knew how to express myself because it was such a personal thing that was happening to me. I was unable to talk about the situation or let anyone know what was happening with me, save for my immediate family and friends. And when I say that, it's like 5 people in total. No extended family or acquaintances.

My body was going through some very personal stuff. Some deep and embarrassing stuff. My body was going through changes as a woman, and I was reluctant to speak of it to other people. It was my woman things that were going to get overhauled and changed, and I didn't want people to look at me differently.

I didn't want to be known as that person who has cancer. I wanted them to know me for who I was, not what I was going through. I didn't want special treatment. I just wanted to do what was necessary to get myself better. To listen intently to what was being said and offered to me, and make a decision based on what I felt God was telling me to do.

I listened and followed the steps that were presented for diagnosis and for plans of action. I feel as if the Lord put me in touch with just the right people at just the right time. It was and has been a road of healing, and although I am healed, I believe that every day gets better. More is coming out that is helping me to be whole. That was my goal, wholeness.

It happens all at once, and it happens on the journey of our lifetime. God gives us the boost to get over, and then the plan and the strength for each piece of life that comes.

We are constantly becoming whole. Spiritually, physically, emotionally, and relationally. All areas are being worked on. Sometimes we feel like we are being squeezed so hard that we're going to burst. And, like the tangy, tart, and cleansing juice that comes from a lemon, we get cleansed and strengthened to be able to go forward. I love lemons and believe that they are good for us. So is the squeezing. Sometimes you have to be squeezed so that the beautiful juice inside you can come out to cleanse you and bless others.

I don't believe that God does all the squeezing. I believe that we also open ourselves to things that cause us pain. Our words and thoughts play a major part in what happens in our lives. What we say and think matters. How we see ourselves matters. That is a big thing with me, and I know it is with many others. It is also in many places within the Bible, which I believe to be the ultimate truth.

So... back to the journey.

A Word...

Offense is coming to stop your ascent to leadership.

Manage your mind because it will affect your body.

Every one of us wants to have an impact. Strategically position yourself for maximum impact.

October 25, 2020

Focus and Discipline

So, I've been focusing on the "didn't dos" instead of the "have dones" and it's not helping my walk and growth.

Last night as I was preparing for bed, I looked at my collar bones. I remembered a comment my friend made about how skinny my neck was getting.

I then realized that despite the fact that I had been going up and down 5 pounds during this time, getting below 140 and then going back up to 140, it required a tremendous amount of discipline and focus to get to where I was.

I had lost, from my highest weight, 70 pounds, 55 of which were in this past year. I started the quest to really watch what we ate and get on an eating plan this time last year. We got through the Holiday Season... a business retreat, wedding, Thanksgiving, Christmas, New Year, and stuff in between. This entire year, especially during this pandemic, we have been continuing with this process.

We've gotten low, and we're only about 20 pounds away from our goal. We kept going up 5 and coming down 5 so as not to get beyond a certain point.

I realized the intense discipline involved in this and where it was taking us. We have been working together. Working out and eating as best as possible to continue on this journey. Our goal is to finish up by the end of this year and then continue in maintenance.

Despite the fact that we're going up and down by 5, I have to remember where I came from... what I've already accomplished and not throw out what I've done for what I'm currently doing.

Sometimes, while you're on a path and you've reached a certain goal, you take a little break. If you take too long to continue on the path/plan you've mapped out, and linger too long on the break, you may not have the energy to continue on to the final goal. It's just a law of inertia. It's okay to rest for a minute and take a small break, but lingering there too long will cause you to lose momentum and make it more difficult to maintain focus and cross the finish line.

So, now to take that to other parts of life. To transfer it to the businesses and daily things.

I got a new planner a couple of weeks ago and I've been logging my gratitude every day. I put a picture of myself at my new weight and a couple of Post-its with the goals I want to reach by the end of the year, and I'm looking at them every day. I also need to get a picture of what my bank account will look like.

The wedding is coming up in three weeks, followed by another one the day after Thanksgiving. So... get on track for the first one so I'm 135 by then and after that wedding, get back on track for the Thanksgiving one. That one is going to be interesting because Thanksgiving is on a Thursday and that wedding is on a Saturday. That leaves one day, Friday, to get it together, so I feel well for the wedding as I'm doing the makeup for the bride and want to be at the top of my game. Then fully back on track on Sunday or Monday until the upcoming Holidays... Christmas Eve, Christmas, and New Year's.

This year, for the Holidays, I want to do things differently. I don't know that I want to go through everything I went through last year. It was great cooking healthy meals, and if I cook, I'd like to do that again. I wish this year we were going somewhere, and we could just have a little plate and go home. That is my prayer for this whole Holiday season. It's easier to do that and stay on track than it is to make the whole meal, have leftovers, and eat them for days.

I don't know. I just don't feel like having a bunch of people over. I want to continue on my quest. Unless the entire blessing comes in and we're in a position to be somewhere bigger and have our stuff together to be somewhere else and ugh... I don't know. You know my heart, Lord. My desires are before You.

I am believing for a crowning year, like you keep reminding me of. For it all to be over and to be walking in the Scripture 3 John 2, prospering in all areas of life, like it never happened.

November 22, 2020

Scale Rules

Does the scale rule your day? I am working on that. How I live my day and what the number says has a lot to do with what and how I feel that day.

I am learning that with the food intake, there are certain feelings that come with it. Depending on what is consumed, it brings on different things. I am just sharing what I feel when I consume certain things. They all affect the body differently.

So, I'm learning to live within these parameters. I want to enjoy what I'm feeling during this Holiday season, and I want to enjoy the company of my family and the foods they make that remind me of the days when I was young, and my tight-knit family was around.

What do I do? I make up for it in other ways. On the days that I know I've indulged a little bit more, I will not weigh myself. I will just adjust the food intake to make up for it so that I am stable and then weigh myself when necessary.

The important thing is to keep a handle on it so that it stays within reach and not let the numbers dictate what's happening, but what you consume to let the body heal itself and make it run more efficiently.

November 26, 2020

Today was Thanksgiving. It was a fairly good day. I am so grateful for so many things. This year has been like no other. Every year pretty much is, but the whole world was in a state of quarantine, like every patch of the beautiful blue and white ball was sick.

I am grateful that we are healthy and that we have the Blessing of the Lord operating in your lives. That is the most wonderful thing we could ever have.

I have to apologize to the Holy Spirit living within me. With all the things we have been doing to change our bodies, eating Thanksgiving dinner was totally different than it ever was, but during our meal and right afterwards we were both a little sick. Not in an unhealthy way, but so full that we couldn't believe that the same size plated meal that we ate last year was making us fuller than ever this year.

We got so full so fast and felt so crummy... both of us were hurting... I thought I was going to explode!!

November 29, 2020

Today I was studying the life of Abraham in Genesis 12-14. I was amazed at his obedience. He followed the Lord on just a few words and uprooted his family to follow Him to a land that he hadn't seen yet.

Where am I in my obedience? Where am I in the plan of God for my life right now? Am I supposed to be in leadership, leading people? How can I follow?

Then here we are… the same thing still here after all these years, the binging, dysmorphia, purging, and general desire to self-loathe. I want to know where this is coming from. It's been a year of great things. Even in this pandemic, I have had somewhat of a handle on this thing by keeping my thoughts and feelings in check through journaling. Maybe I haven't, I don't know. All I know is that I've eaten maybe a week's worth of calories in one day. Maybe it's what everyone does around this time of year?

I don't want to. It's nice to have a meal here and there, but losing total control like this is not good. I am inebriated, not with drink, but with food and sugar. I guess you can say I'm no better at this moment than an alcoholic who has just taken a drink after being clean for over a year. It makes me think of my brother, who we've now lost track of. We know he's in a hospital, but have no clue what is going on, and we can't seem to get a straight answer from anyone.

My Lord. I need to get a hold of things in my life. I need to get my areas in order. With long life will

He satisfy me and show me His salvation. (Psalm 91:16 NKJV).

The binging comes from thinking that you are going to start fresh and never fall again. That you can handle just a little and it's all going to be OK. That you can get it all lost and never have to think about it again. Welcome to Fantasy Land!

December 5, 2020

Ever been so upset with someone who refused to change their life? And then you looked in the mirror and saw yourself? I'm mourning my brother. I cannot believe it, he's gone. And yet, there's a part of me that understands it. I'm no better, I've gone off the rails and headed down a path I definitely don't want to be on, and if I don't acknowledge that I'm lost, I'll be on this road longer than I'd like, and it will take me even longer to get back. These irritations blind me to God's blessings and grace.

December 14, 2020

No one seems to understand how we are all feeling. Maybe they do, maybe they don't. I am not sure how they can just let things go like this.

They're not clear on when or where it took place, what happened, or what the thing was that led to his demise. Cousins, aunts, medical people, no one knows or is saying much. It feels like hearsay in a court case; none of it was admissible.

Today we received the pictures from the funeral home as his body was picked up from the hospital. They handled him so well. Just like my prayer!!!

I made a prayer request sheet for the Lord...
Treat him with dignity.
Safe and blessed transport.
He is dressed well and gently.
He looks well.
Every detail is in order, and there is no delay.
All who are caring for him and responsible for him from hospital to tomb are blessed of the Lord.
That we have a proper video that we can watch.

All details we cannot take care of are handled.

Grazie per tutto l'aiuto che state fornendo a me e alla mia famiglia. Quando pensate che avremo la fattura per la sepoltura nella cripta di famiglia?

Sometimes to say things in my native language goes so much deeper within my heart and spirit and makes it more meaningful to me.

Translation....

Thank you for all the help that you're providing to my family. When do you think we will have the proper paperwork to put him in the family crypt?

...Take the pause that refreshes....

What compound effect do I want to finish this year with that will catapult me to the next and carry me abundantly through it?

Go someplace physically or within yourself every day to change the current image and build the desired one.

What images do I want to build for this year?

At first look on a day like today... I want to be more than I am right now. I am looking at the end of a life, and want to be what I am supposed to be here for - His purpose.

I'm realizing I cannot make the same calls as before to receive the same type of compassion, because there are so many precious ones that have left this world and gone to their heavenly home. Maybe you thought it was good at the time, and now I need something else, and I am OK with that.

The one person who totally paid attention and gave me the responses and guidance needed is no longer with me, and although there are several who are still here that I am grateful for, things are not the same. I don't know, grief is just weird.

I want to dance. I want to feel good. I want to teach others how to dance and feel good. I want to teach them how to be at peace and find that peace in You... as I did just now. It was awesome!

The torment that took place before is now quashed, and he is at peace. I am so grateful that he is with You and no longer in any pain. So grateful he is safe in Your arms and that his earthly body is almost at rest with the family that is waiting for him there.

I want to be on that journey with him… as he's making his final drive through town on his way to the church, as he's being brought in for his final service, and then being brought into the chapel at the cemetery. That would mean so much to me. I cannot even say. I just pour my heart out to You Lord!

I can't play the music loud enough in my ears! I wish there was a way to make it so loud in my brain that it drowns out everything else. Musical therapy!

It's great that I can sit here and type. Awesome that this device was able to be paired, so I can do both at once!! Music and getting it all out.

Life will never be the same, life is changing!!!

What happened today… a missed call that turned into a good conversation, which allowed me to share my requests for help and prayer with the matter at hand.

A message that is just right for this time, as this year is coming to a close and I am believing for BIG THINGS to take place that will blot out all of our transgressions like no other year… that there would be such a restoration physically, spiritually, emotionally, and financially… like we have never seen before… like nothing evil had ever happened. For the Lord to set back the clock, as if no lack had ever happened, and there to be no smell of smoke… just like the three Hebrew men in the furnace… and one like the Son of God walking with them.

What does this look like to me???? For all areas of my life to be in alignment with You! To be able to get back to those things that you've put on my heart before the year ends, so everyone can benefit from it!

For my entire family to be serving You. For them to know the TRUTH and for that TRUTH to set them free.

That would be the crowning of my year. I know James has specific things he wants that he's had on his heart for a long time, and I want the same things too. Blessings and abundance for both of us.

The compound effect... that our bodies would change, get healthier, and reach the weights we desire.

I want the tools and space to promote the wellness that's in my heart. I want a great workout room that I can put in all the exercise equipment I want. One with mirrors and a floor to be able to do aerobics or Zumba... floor workouts as I did back in the 80s and 90s. That would be awesome... to just dance! To be able to freely move my body to my favorite music!

To have a positive and lasting impact on the world that will last for years to come. A legacy to leave behind that will have an overreaching ripple effect.

To be a great blogger and vlogger that has a good, lasting impact on others that leads people to the TRUTH of Christ, changing their lives completely for HIM... that they follow HIM and have peace in HIM, because without HIM, there is no peace in this world.

When I think of you, sweet brother, I think of all the promise that could have been your life. How we both loved music, and the songs we would listen to, and how they affected us.

I think about the time you told me that God did not create me to be a beast of burden, that He wanted me to have a good life, and not be under someone's thumb and molded into their image of me.

Your youth and who you were when you were truly yourself, not when you were tormented, being tempted, and attacked. When you couldn't see straight because the demon's calls were stronger in your mind than the call of the Lord on your heart.

When I listen to music from back in our day, it builds a picture in my heart of the life that could have been for both of us. One of our relationship being truly and fully shared and enjoyed.

There are few pictures of you because you were hardly around. You were in trouble and paying for it, or out there doing your own thing. No one could keep you down. Even when you were physically present, it seemed like you were somewhere else... maybe thinking about where and when the next fix was coming.

As I see you lying there, I think to myself, how different things could have been, and I miss the true chats that we used to have... when you were honest with us and with yourself. That is the person I remember, that will be forever in my heart, and that I will miss. This is the brother I choose to remember.

I pray that you were not in pain during this time. That somehow your body was numb and wasn't feeling what was happening to it, and that your mind was at peace and in the presence of Christ.

I would like to think that you were not in pain or struggling alone without hope. I pray that the joyful conversations we had were the memories that were going through you. Those wonderful memories of peaceful and loving days were what were playing in your mind. That torment was far away, and that your sins and unpleasant memories were not what was at the forefront.

There are so many things I want to say to you. I know I can tell them to you now and that you will hear them, but I will not hear you. I remember your voice and how you would laugh.

What I think now is that people will feel that you are no longer a burden to them. They feel badly that you are gone, if that, but I know there are those who are grateful you are no longer here, causing them unrest.

They knew who you were, in good times and in bad, and I know that they loved you deep down and may have been a little afraid and even tired of the other side of you. That part makes me sad.

Take a look all around, and I will be there. When in Rome 😄 The lead singer looks like you a little!

I want to travel there in freedom and be able to move about in my own way... in a way pleasing to God and to me. In a peaceful, realaxing way, being able to see what I want and with who I *want. You know... without obligation to others. That they wouldn't even know... that we could enjoy our time and visit there.*

I want to go places that have special memories and share that, and go to new places and make new memories with those I love... without limits... physically or financially!

December 23, 2020

I really wanted this week to be special. To be in incubation and cocoon mode while we process what's happened and is happening with my brother.

I am not happy thus far with the way things are turning out. The last I knew, the paperwork to repair the crypt had not been received, and tomorrow is Christmas Eve.

It is so absurd that these people don't have email or a way to communicate in modern society. My jaw has dropped to the ground. I am bewildered. It's unreal to me, and it looks like it's causing a delay.

If they had had smart phones and emails, this would have been resolved by Monday or yesterday. Yet here we are, the day before Christmas Eve.

I am so grateful that my Dad brought us here. Like him, I don't think I'd want to put up with the bureaucracy that goes on over there. They think they have all these rules that are so great, but sometimes all they do is cause undue delays. They have these beautiful tracks, or so they think, because from where I'm sitting, the trains never leave the freaking station and reach their destinations. When they finally do, they're always off schedule, and in a way that is beyond wild.

The frustration feels like an attack of the enemy. Just nuts. From what I heard, they can't skip counties. Yet my aunt is having people over and getting exposed to the virus, and having to quarantine. And a document doesn't get sent out? They have a blank piece of paper, and they're not doing everything they can to get it taken care of properly. Unbelievable!!! All they had to do is see that it's blank and call or email the funeral home to help them fill it out or get the proper paperwork. I just don't get stuff like that. It's crazy stupid in my opinion. Every single experience I've ever had is a crazy paper shuffle for days on end, moving it like they are doing something important, when all they're really doing is moving a piece of paper from one place to another!

I put it in Your hands, and I'm just waiting. I am sorry that I am frustrated. I have to remember that it's in Your Hands and not theirs, and I cannot understand the delay. I cannot understand why. I was really annoyed that it's this close to Christmas. He's been gone since the 2nd of December, and now it's the 23rd.

An email just came in entitled "When God Doesn't Fix It." Goodness! I don't want him sitting there until all their holidays are over. This is so freaking ridiculous. I almost never want to go back there! It's not the place I remember. Their bureaucracy has soured me to the rest of it. I am just beyond this whole thing.

You know my heart, what it's like. Attempting to celebrate the Holidays when this is all undone and up in the air SUCKS!

I have a way of wanting certain things wrapped up nice, with a beautiful bow. Is that wrong? To want something special and wonderful to happen? To have the year truly crowned with all of my prayers answered for now?

Write the little stories... the sum total of them might be the big one.

Meanwhile, back at the ranch, I'm doing my best to hold on to the ground I've taken. I reached a new setpoint at the beginning of November before the wedding. I've gone up almost 10 since then and then lost some, and am now only 5 away from that.

I am saving myself for this Christmas Eve and Christmas and hope to be right back on track afterwards. Getting myself in there, back in the game, and keeping it down in order to start back up in the new year to make the rest of my headway towards the ultimate goal.

What other goals should I be pursuing in this new year? Part of me wants to wait to see how this one ends. What is the crown that is going to be on my year on the 31st?

I'm getting weird thoughts of grief... jump into the grave, screaming, the loss, don't let it get ingrained and deep. Also, as time goes by and you have so many losses, don't let them pass you by because you've had so many and have become numb to them.

December 31, 2020

Year-End Recap

This year was one of the greatest years of my life!

It started off with all kinds of things hitting the fan at once. An accumulation of the past three years coming to a head. Things were popping up all over.

Then it happened. The greatest shift I could never imagine took place. First, I decided to put my words on paper and get them out there. I believe that caused an avalanche of blessings to come. *Just in time! I kept speaking my faith, and things began to happen. Seeds I had sown in previous years were starting to pop up.*

Then, even more took place around me as the pandemic hit. For a while, I felt like I was in a bubble because as things were going on around me, it was not happening to me; just like Psalm 91 says... though 1,000 fall at my side, it will not come near me.

The enemy tried to take my blessings away, but I was on a roll, and although it looked like I had lost a couple of rounds, I was still in the ring. The Lord showed up in a mighty way, like He usually does.

There was a flow, just as I had declared with my mouth. That flow made it possible for things to be taken care of when it seemed like the walls were closing in. Then more came in, and more was able to be taken care of, and the words I spoke were being manifested.

Then came the biggest manifestation of all, one day, the seeds I had sown, some from years ago, the ones that I had put on paper that were in my field, as a remembrance to the Lord and for myself, and as a reminder for the enemy to see that they were in the ground, came in like a flood; like the windows of heaven blew open, the blessings came pouring down, and all things were taken care of.

All the years the locust had eaten had been taken care of in abundance, like only God could supply, and with no smell of smoke on us.

I am so excited to have all of these things happen in a time when there was a pandemic that struck our world. In a time where there was famine, the Lord provided for us in ways that could only be marks of His hand.

Only He could bring all these things to pass in our lives and position us to owe no man anything but love, to live the life of John 10:10, in abundance and having more than enough to sow and bless others.

2020... a great year!!!

January 4, 2021

The new year has been here for a few days now and I'm sitting here today, having accomplished a few things this morning, relaxing in front of the TV.

I got up early, did my workout, took my shower, put the laundry away, and did my Bible Study. I've had my green tea, cider drink, made breakfast, had coffee, sent an email, and checked on my brother's progress.

They say it's raining there. I checked the weather, and it is. The only day that is free of rain is Thursday. God, I am angry and annoyed. This is getting ridiculous. Do they not have a darn tent that they can put over the crypt to do the work??? Maybe the rain will get in anyway, since it's open and it would jeopardize the inside? I don't know. I feel like the more questions I ask, the more annoyed they're going to get with me. Are they waiting to open everything until the rain stops? Who has a clue? I'm over here, and they are over there.

I was reading today about Abraham and how he asked questions of You and kept coming back with questions regarding the people in Sodom and Gomorrah. Because he was Your friend, You helped him through the process of his asking. You listened to all his questions and were gracious to him.

Thank you, Lord for indulging me as I ask all these questions. I'm feeling like it's best to ask them here, privately, in front of You, then to ask them there.

Despite what I've accomplished so far, I feel a little lost this morning as I have no goals within me, nor the strength and bandwidth to carry them out. The only thing I can think of is the situation over there and the waiting.

Believing to get my prayers answered quickly.

January 10, 2021

"I'd just like to be there when we get to where I'm going." Be present where you are.

I thought if I just started writing, I would have peace and better direction.

So, I feel like a terrible soldier. For over 3 weeks now, I've been in a state that I've never been in before, and yet, it's all too familiar. I've been quiet, off social media, and just wanting to keep to myself.

The familiar part... getting to a goal and then sabotaging it, losing the progress made. Not sure why I keep doing this. It was just the Holidays, and then just another meal, and now here we are, almost 20 pounds later!

There are a couple of things that are different. My brother is gone, and we're still waiting for him to be buried, and the things that are happening in the country. Because of what happened during Holiday time, I am feeling crappy. I really let myself go. Like I just let go of all restraint.

They are saying some terrible things are going to happen in our nation and that we are to be prepared. At this time, I feel like a terrible soldier of Christ. I have been in a food coma for a while.

Reading a book that is supposed to be like an answer to a problem, and I am afraid to try it.

So, I think this all boils down to fear. To finally realize all that I want or wanted to be, and then, making sure it doesn't happen because then what?

What am I to learn from this? How am I to help others through things like this? Who will listen?

I feel like such a failure. This isn't the first time that this has happened. I thought of it yesterday... it popped into my head... the several times that I had gotten high and then gotten low and changed some major things, only to gain it all back again, and be in worse mental agony than before. I feel crappy right now. I lost so much weight, and then over the Holiday season, I gained about 20 pounds of it back. I want to stop it right now.

I know You want me to slay some big dragons this year. The dragon of weight, the dragon of lack, the dragon of purpose. My purpose. I am thinking of my friend's words and what she sees in me. What the Lord put on my heart and where I was going. The coaching through the Word, the website, and the other parts of life and career.

I knew the Holidays were going to be this way, just wasn't thinking it would be almost 20 pounds' worth. I planned on letting things go and making my way back. I planned on not watching every little thing that I put in my mouth, and allowing myself to enjoy the Holiday season without denying myself what I wanted. Well, I've been allowing myself to have pretty much whatever I want, and now here I am, making my way back from a longer trip than what I thought... I am further away than I had planned to be. I am taking the long way home.

Most importantly, I think right now, it has put me in a drunken state, where I feel that I am not as vigilant as I was before, and not as in tune with the Lord, and what is happening in the world. I prayed for certain things to take place with my brother, and everything was going well until certain circumstances, laws, and people in my family caused delays.

I was not happy about it. Then Christmas and allowing sugar back in, along with other foods and how they are prepared, and getting out of hand with it in more ways than I can think of.

I want to change my life, be part of the prayers of intercession for what is happening in our country, spiritual warfare in the world, and what is going on around me.

I heard a sermon about the madman of Gadara the other day and how he would cut himself. I feel like with every little thing I eat that isn't part of a good plan is me cutting myself. I saw myself doing that in my spirit when I heard about it.

James is doing better with things than me. He is having less sugar and controlling what he eats. Even the healthy treats we've gotten, he's having only half, not as much, and not eating them after a certain time of day.

I am not allowing the electricity in my brain to get to the frequency it needs to be at and to stay there long enough to make the change that needs to happen in my life.

I have made minor changes, but they don't feel permanent and as if I'm making the progress I want. Making a list of wins for myself and going from there.

Real quick...
Freedom in business and a lot of other areas of life
Health - 75 pounds down
New attitude towards the Word and more knowledge of it
New business ideas

The spirit of gluttony is like the spirit of alcoholism. It has the same effects... as a drink affects an alcoholic, so does eating unhealthy trigger foods, and not stopping affect someone with an eating disorder.

So... I am not in control when I am not watching what I put in my mouth. When I am in control of my weight, and I am winning in that area, then I feel like I am winning in other areas. I hope that makes sense because to me it is ridiculous that it has that much power. I guess when I control my eating, I control my body... I buffet it as the Apostle Paul said.

Things I need to remember that will help me...

I can always buy something that will be a treat and eat it, and I can buy it again if I want it. It's available to me, and it's not disappearing, never again to be available for purchase and consumption. I don't have to buy something and think to myself, I am NEVER going to eat that again once I'm done with it.

This new lifestyle is my life journey, not something I am going to do for a little while and then I'm done.

The trip I took to get me here is not going to be the same path that I'm going to be on the rest of my life. And, just because I took that path doesn't mean it's the only path, and I don't have to do the same thing once I'm done.

What got me here is not what's going to keep me here. I can have stuff when I reach my goal, in moderation, and remain stable.

I need to remind myself that there is a 5-pound leeway that is OK, but not beyond that. Sugar will bring me a pound or two over. A little too much salt will do the same. A recipe that isn't completely free of 'whatever' can do that as well. Having a little pasta will do it too. So... all of these things can cause a little fluctuation, and it's normal. It's part of life.

Somewhere along the line, I thought that once I arrived, I'd be done and that would be it. With many things in life, it's not about just reaching the goal, but maintaining it and then setting new ones. Kind of like binge and purge. I don't think I'm supposed to live every area of my life like a bulimic.

Just because you see yourself as a grasshopper doesn't mean that is how they see you. Your perception is not theirs.

I am not without hope and not without control! I am totally in control, and my hope is in the Lord. I am in control of my choices.

I want relief, and I want it fast! In the past, just getting in the game quickly after a fall helped me to practically erase the situation as if it had never happened. That is what I'd like to do this time as well.

I am thinking of the dresses that I just added to my wardrobe, and I am so looking forward to wearing them soon. They are pretty and new, and I know they are going to look great on me. There isn't much that I've put on, and it hasn't been on me for long, so if I just get with it quickly, I can move forward quickly.

We talked about what we're going to do during this time, and we decided that we're going to watch this coming week and finish stuff that we need to finish. Then next week we can start our two-week program to get things started. I am not familiar with the new program that I've been reading about, and putting it together during this time is a little wracking right now. I want to do the new plan. I checked out all of the books, and I really like the recipes. I agree with the method and with the research. I believe it is an answer I've been looking for, and that God sent it to me as a help during this time.

I want to do the following things... get my brother buried this week. Get the week started by scaling down with food and eating a certain way to finish some of the foods that have been in the fridge. Maybe some of that fish… making some recipes that will make it easier to eat the food.

Questions and myths going through my mind…

Who told you that these foods are bad for you? Who told you that you can't eat them and that they are bad for you and will make you fat? Who told you that if you look at certain foods, you will get fat? Who told you that you have to eat everything right now and get it out of the way?

BOTTOM LINE… I THINK IT'S ALL ABOUT THE FREQUENCY….THE FREQUENCY IN YOUR MIND AND WHEN YOU ARE IN THE ZONE, YOU ARE IN A GREAT SPACE, YOU ARE STRONG, AND CAN CONQUER EASIER THAN WHEN YOU ARE NOT… AND YOUR ENERGY AND MIND ARE IN A STATE OF VULNERABILITY WHERE YOU CAN BE SWAYED, AND IT'S NOT AS EASY TO STAY ON TRACK.

January 11, 2021

Some notes from a sermon for good confession/proclamation for wholeness in life.

Confessions of doubt shut the Father out.

Translate what is in the Word into a confession to increase your faith.

The Father will be to you what you confess Him to be.

Isaiah.... The Word does not return void... 55:11

Do not annul the Word by your negative confession.

Wrong confession is a desperate enemy.

Dual confession (positive followed by negative) wipes out the Word you just confessed.

No salvation without confession.

What I confess I possess.

The enemy is the author of sickness and lack, and everything that goes against the Word of God.

If I confess lack or sickness, I am bound by it... I am bound by whatever I confess because my words go out and they do not come back unless I bring them back.

Your confession either glorifies God or the enemy. Either hope or the circumstance.

Possession comes with confession, and possession is kept with continued confession until what we profess is possessed, going from the spiritual to the natural.

Your confession is your faith in words.

Unbelief grows with a negative confession.

My spirit always responds to my confession.

Your confession is your present attitude towards the Father.

Your confession either honors the Father or the enemy of your soul and gives the Word or the enemy dominance in your life.

You rise or fall to the level of your confession.

Learn to hold fast to your confession in the hard and challenging times.

Confession with thanksgiving always brings possession.

An affirmation is a statement of fact or a supposed fact.

Faith and unbelief are built out of affirmations. The affirmation of a doubt builds unbelief. The affirmation of faith builds strength in a believer.

When you are convinced within yourself that the Word of God cannot be broken, you are convinced that the Word and God are one. When you trust in the Word, you are trusting in God and the Father. You affirm with your own heart that the Word of God and the integrity of God are according to the pattern of His Word.

When you trust in the Word, you are trusting in God the Father. You affirm with your own heart that the Word of God and integrity of God is according to the pattern of His Word. Abraham acknowledged that God would make good on everything that He said.

I am who God says I am, I have what God says I have, and I can do what God says I can do.

His Word is your contact as well as your contract with God. Your word can become one with God's Word, and His Word can become one with your word.

His Word abiding in you gives you authority in heaven.

John 15:7

Our confession either imprisons us or sets us free.

January 16, 2021

When you're hungry…. what are you hungry for? All the food in the world will not fill that kind of hunger. It's something so deep that you cannot eat it away. A certain type of food will not satisfy that hunger. No amount or type of drink will quench that thirst that is in your soul.

January 18, 2021

Using past failures as the seed for tomorrow's defeats is a poor waste of the garden of life God's given us.

My brother just wandered from one place to another and never made a go of it anywhere.

SOLACE ON THE MOUNTAIN....

For a while now, during this time, I've been finding solace in shows that I couldn't watch when I was younger. TV shows from the 70s that depicted a simpler time... or so it seems from where I'm sitting at the moment. Simpler in that their lives were simpler, and in a way that seemed more innocent. You didn't have gore, sex, and craziness rampant in a movie or show. They were times when families stood together. When there were morals, and people lived lives *that were simpler than they are today. They were complicated for their times… food, disease, and other things. However, love and peace prevailed above all things.*

I've been hiding in them and seeking peace through them. I am so enjoying being cocooned in them, and am so grateful that I can see them and relive another time in my life that seems to have been lost. I remember certain things and not others. TV was not allowed back in the day in the same way that it is allowed today.

The things that they used to watch, I was not allowed to. Even life in general was different for me because of where we came from and sometimes it was "us" and "them". They would keep us from things that others were doing because they were unfamiliar with them and not appropriate for us… the way our culture was and how our religion dictated.

I'm now finding that some of the things from back then are not as bad as they were played out to be. As I'm watching them now, I'm finding comfort in those times. I'm learning about history and things that happened during those days that I feel I missed in my little Italian shelter.

The older shows like Little House on the Prairie and The Waltons have offered solace during this time and I'm enjoying sitting under my blanket and watching them, getting to know people from another day.

I'm trying to put what I heard and learned this morning into words. I feel free... my authority given to me by the Word of God. It also encompasses my weight. It's a part of my life and it's a part that God's authority given to me can come in and change this too. I don't know if I'm expressing it properly, but I can use this authority in that area as well.

My metabolism can be revved up, not just by taking care of myself, but by speaking to it and taking authority over it. It doesn't have to be like this for the rest of my life. My weight can be given over to the Lord and authority taken over it. I can use the tools the Lord has given me, in menus and books that have been brought into my path. It's like a new bulb has been lit that brought new light to my life like never before.

My tea bag encouragement for today... let things come to you. What is my ability to receive? Like the widow woman in 2 Kings 4... once there was no other receptacle to receive, the oil stopped.

How can I increase my capacity to receive... how can I get more receptacles to receive what God has for me?

As far as the seed I've sown, the Lord has it before His eyes. I take authority over the seed I've sown. The Lord can give it to me NOW. I don't have to wait forever. He's not waiting for my heart to get right, my heart to change, and for me to have a specific plan for it to come to me. I trust the Lord and I hope He can trust me. He has trusted me with little things when it comes to money and other things in life. He has given me little treasures and I hope that I've done right by Him.

What came to me this morning is letting things go... to trust the "Lord that sees" and will see to it that it comes to fruition because He has to be true to His Word. Seed time and harvest will remain, 30/60 and 100-fold. Plenty more to put in store until we hear more. For whatever is not written down, the Lord will show me what to do with it because we can park it where He tells us, and we will wait for further instruction. It doesn't have to be perfect, and all figured out. He is just asking for me to obey and trust.

Dead in our trespasses.

Trespass... to enter the owner's land or property without permission... commit an offense against a person or a set of rules... a sin or offense.

What is my "there"... Elijah. When Elijah went to hide, God asked him why he was there... where am I hiding... God then provided through the ravens and the widow.

What do you have?

What do I have that You have given me that I could use to make a difference in other people's lives?

Responsibility... responding to God's ability.

God has anticipated your problem before you had the need… all we have to do is respond.

January 23, 2021

It has been a long and weird day. Joey's body was finally put to rest this morning at 3:00 a.m. our time, 9:00 a.m. Italy time. We were up to watch it and, thanks to modern technology, were able to see it, be part of it, and even record some of it. The silver lining in this whole waiting process is that because of the repairs that needed to be made, he is resting closer to my Mom. You God, are amazing. Only You!

After it was over, I worked out, took a shower, had breakfast, and went to bed. Woke up feeling really weird… the adrenaline was gone, there was peace. I woke up and was so groggy and tired. Just a weird feeling, nothing bad, just different.

I read for a while, had a little something to eat and am doing a marathon of the TV show Signed, Sealed, Delivered.

One of them was about a soldier who did incredible things while in Afghanistan and the impact he had. The sorrow he went through, how lost he was afterwards, and the Lord brought him back. It was so moving. I started praying for all of our troops... that God would protect their hearts, minds, and bodies. That their spirits would be protected, and their lives be made whole. I prayed in thanksgiving for all they do for us.

The more I read of Your Word, the more I see how a proper government should be set up and how it is supposed to take care of its people.

Take care of your hearts because out of them flow the wellsprings of life and life is so beautiful... don't waste a moment of it.

February 21, 2021

Comfort... how am I seeking it? There are things that make me comfy, and they help me to deal with stuff. I remember one time you got into trouble and to deflect from yourself; you shared a deep secret of mine with Daddy that no one knew just to take the heat off yourself, even if for a minute.

So, comfort comes in the way of food for me. I can go back pretty far in my life to figure that out. I'm not sure when or where it started, but I can recall as far back as about 9 or 10 years old.

This comfort helps me to deal with what's happening around me. I like to indulge in stuff I like, and then I like to beat it out of myself through working out or cleansing myself in one way or another. Being thin makes me feel great. It makes me feel like I'm clean, good, and in control. I feel valued, loved, and worthy of good things. I feel like I'm smart. I feel accomplished and professional, like a conqueror at the top of her game. That is what I feel when I'm eating clean and working out and not feeling stuffed to the gills and drunk on food.

I like to eat and then get rid of it. But in my own way. A way that is more of a binge and purge method, but the purge is in different ways. It's through detoxing and cleansing with healthy food or working out. I feel like it's all temporary, like it's never going to happen again, but then it *does happen again. I do it at different times in my life, and then I say to myself I'm not going to take this path again... then I do! I feel like food has a different impact on me than it does on others. Like some people can eat whatever they want and it doesn't affect them physically or emotionally. It doesn't affect how they feel or how much they weigh. I'm not sure why it affects me the way that it does, and I'm wondering why it does, and when it started.*

This past year, during one of the most difficult times felt around the world, I was in control. I was doing great and losing what I had gained over a long time. I feel great. Last year when it started, it was a normal thing. It was a way of life, and I felt good that I was changing my life.

There were no Holidays and events that took place where we didn't jump off and right back on. For some reason, this year, we have been very close at different times and then I go back to gaining. So, we've lost and gained the same 20 pounds like 3 or 4 times. It's crazy. I distinctly remember two other times in life where this happened. Once was in the 80s where I lost over

35 pounds in the summer of my sophomore year, going into my junior year of High School. I did different things and also did yoga. It may have been the first time in my life that I worked out to lose weight and it felt great!

I lost over 20 pounds that summer and went back to school for my senior year, a bit thinner and a lot more confident. I was bullied and picked on a lot in my youth for my weight gain and how heavy I was. Kids can be brutal. I feel that sometimes I carry that to this day. I remember the people who made fun of me and I look back now and I think, what the heck? I don't like talking like this, but some of them were just ugly, mean, and nasty people inside and what made them think that they had one up on me and could bully me is beyond me.

So, I lost all that weight and I did it again in the beginning of my freshman year of college and I got down pretty low... 108 and then I gained it back. I started eating buttermilk biscuits from the pop-open pack with butter and jam and I couldn't stop myself. I just went from there, to my gaining most of it back. I had been taking a drink form of food whose name I cannot remember at the moment. I do remember one was like a chicken soup, and those powders became my liquid meals.

Then I tried a metabolism diet years later... lost 45 pounds with that specific meal plan, eating healthfully, and I felt great. I had to work out a lot and got down to 115. Then, one night I was working late at a part-time job. They had put me on the schedule late... where I had to clean the equipment, especially the shake machine, and I took one lick of the shake and it did me in. I went home and ate half a bag of Chip Ahoy cookies that were in the cupboard and I don't know what afterwards, but I just kept eating. I wanted to have some treats like other people did and feel "normal" eating a snack and try to be normal like others who could eat and not gain weight. To enjoy a snack, but I couldn't stop myself.

So, food or treats make you feel normal... but not me. I try to feel normal like others do and, for some reason, I cannot. I try to eat like others and *have normal things, but then I feel horrible and that horrible affects me mentally and physically.*

There are so many periods of binge and purge. Periods of eating and then not eating to make up for what I ate. It was and has been that way for a good part of my life. I feel like when I get into this mode of "I'm never going to do this again," I think to myself, I'm never going to eat this stuff or buy it again. I resolve to get rid of all of it and begin following a good plan and continue it for the rest of my life.

Somehow, I've got to make peace with this and live differently. That food is part of life. I have to manage it like I do everything else. There will be ups and downs, great and not so great days. How I handle and continue from there is what really matters.

I remember being made fun of in High School by two girls in my class. They called me Hoover because I ate fast. They befriended me and made fun of me later. It soon became clear that they were not friends, and if the word was common back then, it would have been called gaslighting. It's weird how it's coming up and out of me right now.

These past few months, before Thanksgiving, I was lower than I had been in a long time. My goal was to get as close to my ultimate goal as possible and because of time, I was able to get down to only 16 pounds away. After the Thanksgiving holiday, and during the rest of the Holiday season, I just let it all roll. It was ridiculous! I got so full just from Thanksgiving. Not just full, but unbearably full. Unbelievably full like never before. Even the year before, I had been able to enjoy the Holiday, get right back on, and get myself on track by just starting back the next day. This year it was different. I couldn't bear how I felt. It was horrible. I was so full, and I felt like I had violated my body... my temple, like never before. Why???

That particular feeling of fullness was ridiculous!! Why was I that full and why did I feel that awful? I had overeaten a little the year before, and I hadn't felt that horrible, physically and mentally full... it hadn't affected me emotionally like that last year. I felt drugged and not in control of my faculties and senses. Worse than inebriated!

Not last year, the last Holiday season. The wedding, the Holiday, the birthday, the Christmas Holiday, etc. Not one of those times put me in the state I was in this Thanksgiving. Could it be that I was secretly dealing with the uncertainty of my brother's whereabouts and all the losses that were taking place around me?

It's all a mindset. There is something in the mind that brings these things about. Somewhere along the line, something happened and food was the trigger or the go-to for comfort after whatever it was happened. Was it being pulled out of the life I was used to? Brought to a new place where I didn't know anyone and couldn't communicate with anyone, or express myself until I learned the language? Was it the assault, and the demand to be quiet, and the threat of death to myself and my family if not done so? Was it the overbearance of family and the premature growing up required while parents were working, making their way in their "new land"?

I have no clue what it was and what made it happen. I just know that it's a mindset and a lifestyle you fall into. It's a way that you see yourself and the image you have of yourself on the inside of you. It's how you see yourself and what or who you think you are. How I see myself and how I react to how I see myself may bring this about. Maybe I see myself as unworthy unless I am at a certain weight, eating a certain way, or doing certain things.

Maybe I feel like I'm not like other people and I don't react the same when I snack, so snacking for me is different and I cannot do it in the same way as the others can. Maybe I am not normal... which is what I've always thought and felt. I have to find who I am in Jesus, and who I am in life. Who I am in His Word, so I can be who I'm supposed to be is what I need to focus on. Who He created me to be and what I am to be in life. People will see me how they see me. What's important is how God sees me, how I see myself, and what I feel about myself in Him.

One moment you are with it and then you are drifting!

Drifting is something I often do. I go somewhere and I don't come back for a while. But when I'm back... watch out... I cannot stop, until I drift again.

What causes the drifting? What causes the stepping back and reclusiveness? Is this going on anywhere else?

The 80s music. It does something to me. What was it about that time? Was it the fact that I had been so "under thumb" while living at home and it was a time that I was finally free to do what I wanted, when and where I wanted, without anyone being there? I was free pretty much to be myself and express myself.

Those songs are like memories of things that were going on at that time. I can listen to a song and it will take me there. Then, there is that time I met up with you Joey to talk about something that was happening... a situation that I talked to you about first before anyone else. You said God didn't make me to be a beast of burden. That this was weighing me down in the wrong way and it was OK to want to be free.

There was something about you... and as I look back, I see that if things had been different, you would have been a more consistent rock for me.

The thing that destroyed you will not destroy me. I want to live my life with the type of consistency that the Lord would be pleased with, that will give Him glory, and that will allow the Holy Spirit the proper access to my life.

Since the beginning of time man has been trying to keep his body under submission from one thing or another. We have been managing our desires, controlling our lusts, keeping our bodies intact so that they age gracefully. Trying to maintain a balance either chemically or physically. Keeping track of our actions so we behave and are in check with all areas of our life. Some of us try harder than others to maintain this balance. To some it comes easy, and to others it is more of a challenge. Some take time to unravel and can take a lot of hits. While others, the slightest tipping of the scale one way or the other will cause the imbalance that will lead to an avalanche.

Why are some more susceptible to change than others? What makes one person more likely to get off balance by the little things than another? Why does one person's equilibrium take a mountain of heap to make them topple and some can succumb to the littlest piece of dirt thrust on them? Some can have chaos around them as they live life and not much rattles them. Then there are others where the slightest little upset in schedule, chemical, physical, sunshine, rain, etc. will set them off. The littlest of imbalances will cause them to act differently. One circumstance, one meal, one cup of tea, one strange word can cause one to keep going and one will cause others to make a huge difference.

February 22, 2021

Today is the first day of the metabolism restart and I am trying to keep myself. I woke up late, didn't want to do my workout, and I'm getting called to do stuff, and I want to work out before I go anywhere. Just sitting here not wanting to move or work out... trying to plan meals. 😡

February 27, 2021

So… a couple of days ago, I was listening to some music that brought up some memories of past relationships. I asked the Lord to please remove any shred of soul ties that may be lingering around.

I had a dream about my Mom. I was fighting the urge to wake up so I could spend more time with her. I felt like I was split in two because I didn't want to leave her presence, but I woke up with that feeling of being torn and missing her.

As I think about the dream and all that happened, I realize that maybe my Mom came to help get rid of these soul ties. Was my Mom coming to let me know that we were being washed clean of what we had done and taken care of things spiritually for us? Like the soul ties are gone? There was so much symbolism in that dream. I know Jesus has washed away all my sins, but I was concerned about those ties… wanted to make sure they were broken.

I wish I had more time in the dream. I wanted to be in my Mom's presence longer. I wanted the feeling of her to stay with me a bit more. That warm feeling she exuded when she was being especially loving and wanting to tell you something important.

I know people are connected to music and certain music brings about memories. The tune takes you back in time and brings about feelings and memories from that time in life. You're back there in a flash. Just with a few notes, and you start reliving that era like you never left.

Managing the traveling back and forth is to our best advantage. We need to be able to listen and have a healthy going back and coming forward. Take the best parts of the memory and what you learned from it. Hug yourself so that it's a good experience and the song becomes a good memory, not one that brings depressive tears. Let it be a nostalgic remembrance. Come back so you don't get down in the dumps and go down a rabbit hole that will leave you worse than Alice... not coming back.

March 3, 2021

In your attempt to make yourself look bigger, make sure that you are not making others smaller while recounting stories of what is happening in your life.

I'm watching all these new shows and all the controversy they are showing... all the crazy stuff that is going on in the world. Everything is included... anything you can think of. That's why I'm liking the older shows better!

I want to make a change in this world. So tired of all this "cancel" stuff and people feeling under-cared for and unacknowledged. There are so many that need Jesus and to know the truth.

I am so at peace with where I am right now. At the same time, I know you want me to increase. Following what you have for me is the way to increase. I am having flashbacks of things people have said to me... that the world needs me so I can use my voice... a platform. To be a lighthouse to those drifting on dark and stormy seas.

What do you want me to do? I'm so in love with your Word and with sowing and reaping, wanting to share the Word and the love you've shown me.

What should I do? Where do you want me to start? I haven't been in the loop for so long and I am just out there. I need to rein myself in and get with it again. I just want help from You and not the voices of others and where they think I should be.

March 8, 2021

When you stop using faith, you stop being fruitful and then you have to go to Egypt (the world) to get what you need instead of the Kingdom of God.

To fail to increase is a violation of your Covenant.

March 15, 2021

It's the last week of the metabolism restart. I am feeling very well, my skin is very taught and supple. I've lost 11 pounds so far. I was hoping to lose 20 on this... it says up to 20 in the book and stuff. If we don't lose the desired amount, they suggest doing another round until we get within 5 pounds of our goal weight.

I believe that I can get this done. Sometimes, there's a looming memory of the words of my physician in CT. I was talking to her about weight loss and shared my ultimate goal with her. Her response was, "that's a pretty lofty goal for someone your age." Somewhere I stored that.

I was hoping this plan would reset me and give me the metabolism I've desired. One where there isn't a major repercussion for every little splurge.

I believe I'd like to continue for another round... that would be another 4 weeks and it would take place during Easter season. I'm OK with that. I'll be finished the Sunday before the memorial service for Mama Sue. If I lose another 11 pounds, that will put me at 136, which is where we left off right before Thanksgiving and I'd still have another 15 or so to go. I was really hoping to get to 115 and have 5 pounds to play with, but how long will that take?

Maybe after I do the other round I can quit for a little bit and just add simple stuff and see what happens and maybe go back on in May. I don't know. I am peaceful and happy with this plan. The hardest days for me, I think, are the two protein days... only because of the snacks. I'm hoping to get more books so I can see more recipes and options.

Those 6 day a week, almost two-hour workouts were feeling like I wasn't getting the job done. Then I felt like if I didn't do the workouts, I would never be able to maintain it. It was like being in bondage... a slave to the workout with the results that I'm getting now. This plan doesn't make me feel bound and, on a treadmill, going nowhere and I'm enjoying the workout plan now.

The every two day split, is working well for me. It feels good to have it broken up, two days of cardio, weights for 2 days, and then the lighter, aerobics, Pilates, or walking, etc. for the following 2 days. Plus, you've got different types *of music and mindset for each one. Meals in the mornings because of the snack right before the workout, which is also nice. For me, besides meal prep and getting familiar with the new plan, this way is much more peaceful. James doesn't like it as much. I think it's because he really enjoys more traditional breakfast foods. He won't be continuing on with me during the extended period. He says he'll support me… so I can make pretty much everything on the menu and he can add to or alter what I'm doing.*

Differences I'm seeing… water is easier to drink, I have more energy, and my density is healthier, which makes me feel stronger.

March 17, 2021

Yesterday was a busy and productive day. I got a lot done. I was tired and prepped two meals. One for our dinner and one for 2 other days. It took a while, and I was tired. It was warm. It's been getting warm the past few days and then it's going back down. Praise Jesus.

I got two new cookbooks and I'm looking for more recipes and ideas to eat healthy and innovatively. I'm excited!

Tried on some dresses that I got back in November and took new pictures since I forgot to measure myself when I started this new plan. I was about 12 pounds lighter than I am right now. I thought with this new plan I would look good in them since my body has been changing, but 12 pounds less back then and 3% body fat since then, and they look good.

This morning's workout was different. It seems like each week the way I feel changes because of what's happening inside. I can feel the change in my fat ratio and in my arms and legs. My skin is tighter and I feel more in tune when I work out. I feel a change in the way my muscles feel as I'm exercising them and it's easier to move. I really feel each muscle working when I'm concentrated on it. It's a great feeling! I'm focusing on the positive and trying not to think about the fact that the four weeks will be up in a few days, and that I'm still 31 pounds away *from my goal, and I'm not sure if I should start another round or not.*

So now... what do I do? Do I see it through and continue on this journey? I can feel the muscle building, and it feels good, and I want it to continue. The two toughest days are the proteins days and weekends are my favorite. That's when we get to have everything, and I really like the meals on that one... there's more freedom and fewer food restrictions.

The book says up to 20 pounds and if you're losing at least 3.5 pounds a week, that is good. At this point, I've barely lost what I had gained from my original loss. Weird, I know, but all in all, it's more than 3.5 a week, so that is good.

I got down to 135 at the beginning of November and then we had the Holidays and I ate what I wanted. I did not restrain myself. I enjoyed myself. So, I wound up at 157 when I started this new plan, which is a 22-pound gain in three months. It will be Easter during the second round, but I will be done before the Memorial Service at the end of April.

I am hoping to have more changes and be back at that weight and fat percentage, if not lower. Maybe I needed this first round to prep to get me going so I can continue and finish. After the second round, the way I'm feeling right now, it will just be recipes and doing different stuff without the phases. Maybe doing the week for once or twice a month. Yesterday I was so weary. There is a lot going on.

March 19, 2021

A wonderful night's sleep… it was cool and comfortable. Woke up to a 3-pound loss this morning. It felt good and I'm trying to figure out how that happened since we've gone up and down the past few weeks.

We both lost 3 pounds and we're wondering what we did. What did we do differently yesterday? I had the chicken bacon for a snack before workout with one and a half bottles of water. Then we had a salsa omelet for breakfast, followed by a stuffed red pepper as a snack, which was actually a lunch instead. Then, we had the soup for lunch and another stuffed *pepper for dinner. So, we had the 5 meals and I think I drank about 5 or 6 waters and two teas for the day, which is more water than I've had in one day on this.*

So, maybe the extra water was it? Not sure, but I sure am excited and will drink more today. We're in my favorite part of the plan... the weekend!!!

March 20, 2021

It's Saturday! It's Saturday! So excited... going to do Pilates and some Bible studying. I have some time to myself and that is going to be a great thing... no matter how long or short.

My mind and body are in a struggle. I am tired and feeling well at the same time. How is that possible? I'm frustrated and I don't know why... almost angry at something, but there's nothing to be angry about. I have a lot to do, and so much to watch to get our recording capacity to a good percentage, and I don't want to get up off the couch... from here to there to rest. I know the past couple of days have been busy, and maybe that is why I feel like a lazy potato... not sure.

There are two days left of this four-week cycle. Then I am continuing on for another four weeks. James is doing two of the four with me, which I'm really excited about. I can see such a change in my body. It's being sculpted into the body I've always wanted for myself.

This struggle is probably because my body is changing physically and chemically. Each workout I've done during these four weeks has been different. Each week it feels different, not the same as the week before, and my body feels stronger and tighter as the weeks go by.

Why do I have these periods of real tiredness? Maybe daylight savings time has made a difference? We'll see what happens as I get into the next few weeks.

Once I get a little lower, I'm going to make an appointment for physicals for us. I want to get into the low 30s before I go back in. It will be neat to see what the bloodwork says and the changes that are there. I'm sure the numbers will be even better than last year!

April 12, 2021

I keep losing the same pound over and over. I gain it and lose it the next day, and then I gain it again. It feels like Groundhog Day in my body. I am not sure why it's happening. I've come to a standstill, and I'm a little concerned that the weight is not coming off.

I have a big event coming at the end of this month, and I only have 2 weeks left to get to my goal of another 10 pounds, and I'm not sure what to do. I'm not deviating from the plan I'm on because I believe that perseverance will alter this cycle and I will have breakthrough. Reminding myself that this is a lifestyle for me.

April 14, 2021

I'm coming up with a new game plan. I have not made any progress with the scale this week. I feel like I'm more bloated and I am not losing weight. So, I've decided to go on my secret weapon plan for a few days... 9 days until we leave to go to the Memorial and then watch myself that weekend.

When I get back, I am going to finish off those shakes, then see where I am, and go back on whichever plan is going to get me to where I need to be.

I know that I really like some plans for scaling down and some for maintaining my lifestyle. These recipes I've learned are awesome. Right now, though, I really want to get down on the scale, get to my goal, and work on maintenance with that plan. I feel like I've been on this journey forever, and I'm tired of being in the same spot for so long.

We started this journey over a year ago. It's actually been a year and a half. In that time, I've only lost 45 pounds. I lost a total of 55 and gained 20 of it back, lost 10 of it, so now I'm about 10 behind the ball.

I bought so much food for this new plan that I'm going to look for recipes that I can make and freeze so that the food doesn't spoil because some of it is not on the current plan I've chosen.

Anyway…. here we go. My goal is 115 by my next doctor's appointment. That means 30 pounds in the next two and a half months. If I have to get really strict for part of the next couple of months, then that's what I'm going to do to get there, and then maintain afterwards.

I want to be done with this, and I know that it's not going to damage my system. I am going to treat myself like a weightlifter that is preparing for a competition that is coming up. I'm going to really focus on this goal. Then, after the competition, I will take another route.

April 15, 2021

I had quite a few things on my "to do" list today that I wanted to take care of, and it felt good to get them done. I felt really accomplished as I crossed items off my master list.

Switching the meal plan for now has also brought a change in the scale and in my body. For that, I am grateful.

Yet, I'm sitting here after a call, and I am going through a little something. Not sure... what is it? I'm wondering about stuff, and I realize that I don't have anything specific written or to set myself to. I have to make a better list of things that need to be done with deadlines. Otherwise, "one day" will never come.

Writing the major things down. Then I'll reverse engineer to execute a more specific plan.

The music devotional... to keep working on that
A plan for the future... other books
Finishing off this weight thing
Look into more training that aligns with what's in my heart for the future.

May 30, 2021

PTSD... is there such a thing as PTSD when it comes to balancing your physical life and a good eating plan? Is there such a thing as having an eating disorder and handling it in a way that makes you go back and forth... a yo-yo thing that makes you afraid that if you get to your goal, something is going to happen... like you're not worthy of the good and healthy body, being thin and wearing nice clothes... like it's a form of success and you're not worthy of it. Someone or something told you that it's not for you. It's never going to be for you, and even if you get there, it will only be a temporary journey for you... like a long weekend or short vacation before you snap back to your old life. Hey Cinderella!

Who said that? Who said... at your age, that is a lofty goal? Who said that you're not worthy of being there? That those things you've wanted to wear are not for you? Let's face it... no matter what size you are, there are certain things that don't look good on us because of the cut, style, or color. You could be a size 2 or 20 and that wouldn't matter.

What's important is that you can reach the goal you want, and you are worthy of staying there.

There isn't a treat or meal in the world that is worth your feeling horrible.

I feel like, for myself, that I get to a certain point and there's a rope that tries to pull me back. Like a fence that goes up that I cannot get over, and it keeps me in the yard. I get to a certain weight, then I see myself in the clothes. Although I'm smaller and feel better, I still feel like I look the same, even if my clothes are smaller. I feel like I look the same in the mirror. It's weird that I don't see much of the progress that's taking place, other than in the numbers on the scale.

I've done this before. I've reached my goal weight several times in my life, and then I binge like crazy and undo all the hard work I've done. One taste of sugar or one good meal and not getting right back on puts me over the edge. I go down a spiral that takes me back to where I was before, or worse... higher than I was before.

Then I try to figure out why I just undid all the hard work, and here I am again, on the same path with a new resolve, a different attitude, but what have I changed inside? What have I changed within me to make my life different and not be the same again? What have I fixed that was broken that will prevent me from going down this road again?

What is it that needs to be fixed so that I do not take another turn down this all too familiar path that doesn't lead me to my desired destination? Why do I feel like I need to eat everything because I'm never going to have it again? Who said that to me? Where did I learn that?

These past few days I learned that there are things that we learn as we're growing up that we may remember or may be deeply rooted, and we're not sure why our behaviors are the way they are. Most of the stuff we're involved in is genetic... a makeup from somewhere in your line and life. However, that DNA can be changed. Those habits can be replaced with healthier ones and rewritten for more positive ones.

What do I remember? Coming here... life changing. Being away from what I knew and was familiar with. Did something happen that I can't remember or that I've stuffed so deep that I don't want to remember? I do have memories of gaining weight, losing it when we went to Italy, and then having my Mom take me to doctors because she couldn't figure out if it was something glandular.

I have memories of eating and getting sick at my first communion... either from eating too much or food poisoning... up most of the night puking. Then, when I went to my grandfather's funeral, which took place during the same trip as my cousin's wedding. I remember my cousin Stella taking me out. We went to a neat restaurant, had great seafood. When I got to the wedding reception that evening, there was seafood there too. I'm not one to leave lobster and shellfish on the table. 🤪

I was up the whole night vomiting and pooping, and even into the next day when we were visiting my aunt Sila. My cousin Roberta was there. I had to keep going to the bathroom... like dry heave poops. Looking back, I'm a little annoyed because this day was the last day that I saw my cousin alive as she passed away just months later. This whole scenario was attempting to steal time away from family because I was feeling less than stellar!

Leave the crap behind and live whatever life it is that feels abundant to you deep within your heart. The one you deserve that Christ died to give you, not the one you feel you have to live because you feel you're less than.

Summer of 2021

Summer was approaching, and I thought to myself, this year, I'm done with watching every little thing I put in my mouth. I want to have a nice summer, enjoying summer treats and having fun when I can.

I don't want to go crazy, but I want a little diversion. What's it going to cost me? I'm hoping not too much and that it won't undo the progress I've made. I'm a little over since I've been treating myself already, but the decision to have some fun, eating things like frozen yogurt, some fritters, and other treats seemed inviting and adventurous.

The nice thing is that I'm liking where I am, and I'm tired of beating myself up. I want to feel normal, whatever that is. I'm tired of the voices in my head that are telling me I'm awful and that the fat around me is the sign of a slob.

All my life, I've felt like I didn't belong anywhere. Like, who I was created to be was this awful, out-of-place thing. Then, through the love of a friend who treated me to some books she had been reading, I felt like they were talking directly to me.

God created me, He loves me, He lives in me, and I am worth something. He has plans, plural with an "s" for me. Those plans are for good and not for evil, to give me a hope and a future.

No more silence, shutting me up, or making me hide in a corner because I'm 10 pounds more than what I want to be, therefore I don't want to come out of hiding.

No more!

I have so many plans that I feel God's put on my heart. Yet I freak out, freeze, and don't move, so nothing gets done because I'm afraid of failing and afraid of succeeding.

I let the voices shut me down. I have ideas, and then I see other people doing them, and I think, "Well, it's already been done, and they're doing so great at it that I probably won't be as good." It's already been done, or whatever. So, I talk myself out of it.

Why do I want to do this? Why do I want to get to that goal? Is it because I feel better there? Is it because it represents a good time in my life? Is it because I was happy in the times I was there? Why do I want to be there? What does it mean for me to be there?

Maybe I want to prove to myself that I can do it again despite what's happened to me. Maybe I want to feel what it's like to be there again. Maybe in my mind, I want to prove that doctor wrong and reach this "lofty goal." Maybe I want to prove to myself and others that you don't have to accept the norm. That with a little effort and focus, you can be at the weight you want, no matter what age or stage in life that you are (barring medical issues that will be a detriment).

I'm watching "My 600-Lb. Life," and I'm wondering what comes first… do they feel disgusting in their bodies so they eat, and then they feel gross, or do they feel gross and then they eat, and it's a Catch-22?

For me, I think in looking back that it started with body shame first. I'm not sure of the reason because I can't pin it on a specific life event. Then you eat because you feel gross, and then you feel gross because of what you've just eaten.

Eating makes you feel like you're in a place that brings you a certain form of ecstasy while you're doing the eating. Then, when you're done, you want that ecstasy again…. that feeling you get when you're doing it, that you want to do it again so that feeling comes back, or you keep doing it so that it doesn't go away.

Eating helps you forget about things while you're in the middle of it, but then I try to remember while I'm doing it that there will be more issues when I'm done, so I can stop myself from going too far, but it doesn't always pan out that way. Once you're done, you still have the issues you ate to escape, and now you have another issue, which is your health and possibly the extra weight and the grossness of what you just ate.

June 12, 2021

Today's spiritual messages were about the mustard seed and also sowing a leap seed. These messages have caused me to ponder, then confirmed a word to me which encouraged me to move forward on my heart's ideas.

I've lost another pound. I know, just one, but I am grateful to be going in the direction I want. I was able to get into another dress!

Last night I thought that if I lost at least 3 pounds a month, that I would be more than done by the end of the year. This gave me peace. I've decided not to get all bunched up in my head for the meals, allowing myself to have a treat every once in a while. Thank you, God, for the peace and the light at the end of the tunnel.

Getting dressed up and having that confidence in myself and in God is what is going to help me move forward on this journey. I want to get out of myself and change the situation.

The Lord has given me oil in this house, and I want to use that oil to get myself out. The oil is me. God has given me gifts with coaching and with my other businesses.

This afternoon I lost a client and friend. It hurts, but I also feel like this is part of the leaping forward process. Sometimes people hurt you. However, in the end, it's really for your benefit that they leave so you're free to move forward to your next level. Like pruning a plant of the dead leaves so that there can be healthier, more productive growth.

I am more than this! My seed is in the ground, and God is not a man that He should lie. My seeds will produce the harvest that I sent them out for. The Lord knows my heart, and He is faithful.

I want to work on my willingness and obedience to have the life God wants me to have. There is work involved in this. There is a lot of baggage with this journey. There are so many unhealthy memories and things associated with this business from the past. I want to change that story and move forward. How do I forget the negative, keep the positive, and change the thought patterns that have been part of my life for almost 40 years?

I have to look at it as a coaching appointment. What would I say to someone who would be sharing something like this with me, asking for my help and guidance? How would I help them to move forward? So, I coach myself in those things.

You are working in me and in my life.

June 14, 2021

This is the first day of a new plan. We're having smoothies and a meal in the evening. It's a fun, Asian-based plan with great dinner recipes.

I am so excited to try new things, and I feel free. A few days ago, I was just sitting, and a thought came to me… if I consistently lost 3-5 pounds a month until the end of the year, that would be about 20 pounds, and I would be at my goal weight. Revisit and hang on to those powerful thoughts. Use them to propel you forward for a great win.

Strategize and plan ahead for Holiday time. Give yourself one day for the Holiday and get right back on the next day! Let's repeat the 2019 Holiday season!

I'm realizing today that the journey really started in May of 2019, when we got our Total Gym. Before that, I had not worked out in over a year. I don't think that's happened since I started working out early in life, except for when I fractured my spine.

Today we went for a walk in a place that we hadn't been to in a while. It was so good to walk around the area and not feel totally exhausted. The last time we walked there, we were both carrying the equivalent of a fifth grader on our backs!

The extra weight was taxing on our bodies. Our backs, knees, feet, and shins would always ache, and we would be so tired when we got back. Today was different. We had more energy, and nothing ached. The same distance we used to cover laboriously before seemed effortless this time.

I am so excited and feel great inside. I'm so looking forward to dinner, trying new recipes, and seeing what this new plan does for the body and scale. This particular one is only for a week. Although it's a little stringent, it's a great opportunity for detoxing, and it's only for seven days. It's awesome!

There are big days, and there are small days. We get to choose what type of day we're going to have.

June 16, 2021

This is the easiest goal I have ever set for myself. While others are experiencing weight gain in their latter years, for me, it will be a time of rejuvenation and of being the healthiest and thinnest I have ever been in my life.

What the enemy meant for evil on Saturday, You are going to turn for good. It is going to be the greatest crossing over ever at this stage in my life. It is going to bring me the biggest emotional, monetary, business, and spiritual blessings ever!

Woman with the issue of blood... in what area of your life are you bleeding and being depleted by?

Faith and tenacity will get you what you want and need from God. Tenacity made her go out and see Jesus, and her faith healed her. Touching God with your faith requires you to make a demand on it for miracles to work in your life.

My heart and mind are in alignment with my faith.

Her faith made her whole! Not just healed, but whole! Whole is the whole thing!!! A restoration, not just the healing of the bleeding, but a *healing of her entire life. Just like the one leper out of the 10, the only one who went back to thank Jesus, was referred to as "made whole." The Word said he was made whole while the others were just healed. I think if he lost anything, like digits or had scars, that the Lord healed them.*

In the spirit of transparency and partnership.

I am cutting edge, not a fast follower.

Do you know or believe you have other options?

The way to increase anything is through personal growth... go through... not just to keep looking at it and dodging it, hoping it will change. Change starts within me first.

Overcome the insecurity of "Can I?"

Overcome the disserving habit you have by developing another, more fruitful habit.

Overcome limitations.

I started, I didn't quit, and I have consistently stayed in motion.

Being uncomfortable is what precedes the next level of growth.

Communicate, negotiate, and lead.

Push through the next lesson so you can see opportunities and rewards.

God's blessing is on the other side of your decision and obedience!

June 22, 2021

One day or one meal? Great morning walk by the ocean and a brief stop at the new donut shop for a little treat and coffee.

After the caffeine and sugar rush from the coffee and treat, I wanted more. Seems like when I have sugar, I want to balance it off with something of substance so I don't crash.

I waited a little bit and just let my body experience the treat. I decided that just because I had a little treat, my whole day wasn't lost. I didn't completely finish the treat, and it was only a cup of coffee with some cream and raw sugar.

So… why make the rest of the day mentally harder to come back from?

Why not stop while you're ahead instead of adding to the impact of things, then making it harder to come back? Sometimes it makes sense to just wait and not let things go down the path that your mind and emotions want you to.

The key word is emotions. Your body may want things, but is it physical hunger or emotional hunger? Emotional hunger can sometimes be so strong that it makes us do things that are unnecessary. There is a healthy path that allows us to handle those emotions. You can choose whether you're going to capture the thought, push it aside and do something healthy for yourself, or you can let the emotion run wild into an area you will regret later. Because then you'll have other emotions to deal with because you overate and now you feel crummy.

June 30, 2021

Compelled and want to eat outside of the plan. Emotional eating occurs due to poor coping skills. Since there is an absence of a healthy replacement behavior, then it will lead to a binging episode.

Ask yourself why you are doing it. The "why am I doing this?" You want to evaluate your state of mind right then. What is it about your environment, circumstances, or thoughts that are making you desire to treat yourself poorly?

What are you running from and running to?

July 8, 2021

The first day you eat to satisfy an emotional issue, and you continue to use food as your feel good, is the start of a pattern that, if not broken, can carry on through your life. It's one meal to another. You keep going and going. Even before you're finished or while you're eating, there's this need for more, because those few moments of relief make you feel better.

With any addiction, something is being covered up, and that is why we use whatever our trigger thing is to overcome that feeling. It can be food, a drug, or a workout. It's different for all of us.

July 2021 - Dysmorphia In Time

Somewhere in time, there was a thought planted. Not sure when or where, but it was put in there and then magnified by someone or something.

I cannot pinpoint the time or the place. There's no doubt it was planted, and boy did it take root! It grew roots all over and barely choked the life out of me. Life as I knew it was different. It had been altered. It had been changed in ways that would have repercussions for years to come.

Despite this significant change, I was not sure of its magnitude or its impact on my life. It became the glasses through which I looked at the rest of the world.

I looked at everyone and everything through these glasses. I couldn't get them off me. My vision was distorted, and I am not sure how to get it back. I saw everyone and everything with a scalpel. With a little knife in my head saying, "If we could fix this or fix that, it would be perfect."

This can refer to a body part, a person, a character flaw, or anything else in life. It's more specific for me in regard to the body, its appearance, comfort, peace, and acceptance. There's a constant quest for perfection, for being a certain way, a specific weight, a hairstyle. Wherever I go and whatever I do, it's all about the presentation, personally and professionally.

As far back as I can remember, I was being bullied. Not so much in my homeland, but here in the States. People weren't very accepting of me. I noticed it more when I started gaining weight. Somewhere from the time we came here, which was in October, and I was put in second grade, to when I entered the third grade, was when things started.

I felt like being the new, international kid was like being under a microscope. My body was doing things I could not control. Things were happening in public places that people should only do in private, and my body was betraying *me, giving people more fodder for bullying. No one could understand what was happening, not even me.*

No one had a clue that certain behaviors are brought on by fear and that fear leads to shame, and that shame leads to outward lashing out. You think it's something that's going to help you and comfort you, but the end result is really not a helpful thing. The very thing you go to for comfort turns your body into a balloon, and nobody likes human balloons that are all blown up and look deformed.

My body was different, my hair was different, my voice was different, everything about me was different. Were they jealous? Did they think their lives were better or worse than mine? What was it about me that was so hideous to them that they felt the need to ridicule me all day long?

Who was I left with? In my adolescence, you told me to watch out for everyone and not trust anyone, even those closest to me. What changed from the time we were home and younger when you left me alone, by myself, thinking it was only long enough for a mass, and that someone would hear me if anything happened, so I was safe? Not too many years after that, it was not OK to be alone or with the wrong company. So, what changed Mom?? Did you know there was a change? Were you aware of it? What were you aware of that changed your mind like that? Man, I wish I could talk to you to find out if there was anything that happened that you became aware of that changed the way you felt about things and about my safety.

July 14, 2021

Hungover today from all the food and sugar from yesterday. Got up later than I wanted and was so sugared up. It's the second day I've gotten up and heard the word discipline. That word got me up, out of bed, and into the workout room.

I'm feeling these past few weeks that getting up early, doing my workout, taking a shower, and having a good breakfast have been good habits. If I do nothing else, I feel victorious. Sometimes

I'm so tired I don't want to do anything else, and at times, it energizes me to do other things.

Motion is something that is essential for my life, even if I'm lying here reading a book or creating some content for my own. Getting words down is also an accomplishment for me. I know that at some point, what I write down is going to be used in some way to help someone in their life. Everyone has something they're known for or famous for. What I want to be known for is speaking loving words into people's lives that shape and change them, giving them wings to fly and a belief that they can be and do what their hearts desire.

Today I'm just sitting here sharing what I'm feeling inside with my little tablet. Maybe I'll share them somewhere, or maybe they will just stay in here. God knows. I'm too tired and feeling strange to do anything else, and so here I am, just typing what is on my heart.

Got to get a handle on this eating thing. Like in the Book, I'm trying to think of eating as worship to God. As taking care of my body. Worshipping Him with what I eat. Even the treats... like rich foods in the Old Testament that were eaten for celebration. Right now, it's a time of celebration. It's Summer Season! Summer always equals fun. A time where responsibilities come to a bit of a halt. It's time to relax, enjoy nature, and things that resemble work slow down, and in some places, completely close up.

There are some memories from my childhood. No school, no work, beach time, special treats, and special bags with treats for the beach. Companies closed for vacation. It was a given. No one was open. Families enjoyed each other and the season... the freedom of Summer! Everyone is getting in on it.

July 16, 2021

I'm reading over notes to put this book together, and I'm reliving some of the entries I made. One I found reminded me of a word I heard towards the end of last year. That You would crown out the year.

So now I'm sitting here, and I'm wondering what the crowning for this past year was and what *the jewels were that were in it. What things made the crown this year? How did it get crowned? I'm trying to remember all the things that would make it as if there were a true crown with jewels in it.*

I don't want to forget one jewel that You put in that crown for me this year. What did You mean by it? What were Your ideas for crowning this year for me? What is the specific crown for the year 2020?

July 17, 2021

Lessons in life… what are the roots and patterns?

There's a root to everything we do. Sometimes the roots are so deep that even we don't know how far down they go or where they originated, who planted them, or how they grew. We keep going back to the same patterns, and we're not sure how we got there. We get to a certain point, and no matter how much progress we make, we tend to get slung back by an invisible cord that snaps and pulls us back.

Working through the causes that have these effects can be just as bewildering as the reasons they came to be. Sometimes it's a veil behind us that keeps things hidden. We only get to see a little shadowy glimpse of what's back there, and we can maybe make it out, but we can't seem to get a clear picture.

So, there's something behind this getting to a certain point physically, emotionally, and spiritually, then taking steps back. I cannot even remember the goal I had at this moment, or the why and how I was able to stay on track for so long.

I was so close. There was so much work involved in getting to my goal and to that specific set point. I finally broke through after grueling months, and now I'm back up again. I need to get back down, get to that place again, and make it the new set point so I can keep going down and finish at my new goal weight.

The zone I was in, in my mind, and the rhythm and vibration I had has changed, and I am praying to get back there.

July 19, 2021

A message popped up on my feed this morning when I was working out. It was an answer from God to a little prayer I prayed yesterday. I wanted an answer to why I'm going in the direction I'm in right now. Last year at this time, I was frustrated because I had been following eating plans to a "T" and it was a struggle to just lose 2 pounds a week.

There was no deviation that I could make because every little deviation cost me a pound. Then it happened. The eating plan I needed crossed my path, and provided relief and moved me to a different set point so I could continue forward.

I scaled down pretty low, past the hump I was at, and then, after reaching the goal for the event we were attending, life stuff happened, and meal by meal, I began to gain. The Holidays were coming, the uncertainty of where my brother was and not being able to speak with him, and then my King of Pain's death.

Life was changing, and the pounds kept accumulating. I was going down and coming back up like a yo-yo. Then there were the Holidays and the uncertainty of burial, and it just kept going.

Listening to this spiritual message, the answer was basically that I have a mission, and the enemy is using food in my life to keep me down. To keep me immobile and feeling horrible so that I'm inebriated, and of no effect to the Kingdom of God. That's what I got out of it.

He's trying to distort my physical image and keep that distortion in the forefront of my mind so that it keeps me from moving forward. This is what I call Groundhog Day... where you can't go forward, can't go back, you're just stuck.

This is not the abundant life at all. This is a wilderness life where you're just going around in circles, not making any progress or getting any closer to the land that God has promised you.

Inside, I was feeling good. I was liking the way I looked and then, he (the enemy) didn't like my progress and started planting thoughts and feelings in me, and I listened, like Eve in the Garden, and started eating and eating. Those thoughts were overpowering me and my desires. At this point, the desire to eat overcame the desire to be healthy, to feel good, and to look good.

That's what's happening every time. That's why I revert when I get close. The enemy is trying to erase the progress I have made and diminish my thoughts and visions of what I want. Keeping me down and out of the game.

There is no way to get rid of the emptiness other than being with God. Food is not going to fill the void. No matter what it is, it's not going to make you feel any better, and it's not going to fix the hole that's in you. Only God can plug up that hole. Only the Holy Spirit can make those changes in you. He is the only one who can fill you up when you're feeling empty. Food is only a temporary fix that leaves you feeling emptier when you're done.

Adversity creates a pattern of behavior, and it fills a need, so you continue with that pattern to fill that need. That pattern is usually destructive.

It's been 8 years since my last major life change, and since then, I've been a little slow. What is it that happened to you that has left you crippled in some form? Have you been crippled in your life? Has an injury or disease wounded you and kept you immobile?

July 20, 2021

The Focus Has Shifted

I can feel myself when I walk now. My knees and upper thighs rub together. I can feel the top part of my belly jiggling. That's 20 pounds now, and it makes a difference.

I like being thinner because I feel better. I didn't want to hide myself, either. When I'm bigger, I feel ashamed I and I don't want to be seen. I'm not sure where that came from. When I hear of an event or somewhere I have to be, I like to be in the best shape possible. I want to be thinner and look better than I was before. I don't know why, I just do. I want to look good for myself. The goal now is to get to the goal weight.

Now my goal is 35 pounds away at this writing (7/20/21).

Keep wanting more? Maybe it's because the food you ate had no micronutrients in it, you got no nutrition in your system, and your body is still hungry for real food.

I don't know if there's a miracle diet out there or one that is perfect for everyone. I've realized that I like having different eating plans and shaking things up a bit. Having options is a comfort for me. When I don't have a meal plan, then I get sidetracked. Having menus, recipes, and ideas on how to eat already mapped out for me helps me to stay on track.

In reading my latest book, I realized I don't have to be qualified, life qualified me. She was so vulnerable in having authored a book and giving people so many tips, but here she was struggling with the exact thing she wrote her book about. So, that being said, I feel so much better, and don't feel like I have to be perfect and when I do, then I have to figure out why and get myself in line.

The things I'm remembering, flashes of things I've experienced...

Deflection... when my brother was caught doing something and decided this would be a good time to out me to my Dad about being bulimic.

That's a lofty goal for someone your age.

You're a disgusting animal.

Remarks like this can only come from someone who's not right to begin with. It started way before we were aware.

The focus needs to shift from losing weight, which implies that somehow your body has gone to a place it should not have, and you need to rein it in and bring it back. This implies that it's a negative thing that needs to change. Whereas, if you shift the focus to desiring to live a healthy lifestyle where you're making better choices to have a longer life span and more energy, at least for me is a better approach. One implies body-shaming, and the other one wants a healthier lifestyle. Such as, choosing NON-

GMO foods and those full of macronutrients, which made me feel better.

What do you want people to say to you when you walk in? Do you want them to say "hey, you've lost weight, you look awesome!" Or, "you're glowing, you look great, what have you been doing?" I realize how much value I place on how people look. For some reason, I'm always looking and comparing to how they looked before... WHY?

Do you want people to make comments that are positive, but what they are really saying is that you looked much better today than the last time they saw you? How do we communicate how people look after we haven't seen them in a while?

I was looking at statistics that say that people who went on diets... 50% of them were more depressed after dieting than those who had not. The extra weight is somehow better than the dieting cycle.

I get it, and I understand it. You've built up a standard for yourself, and maybe that standard isn't what it's supposed to be? I feel like a horse without a bridle right now, running wild in the woods.

We had gotten so far, and the circumstances of life have led me down a path that caused my days to be more self-nurturing, instead of continuing on my quest. It's like a double-edged sword because, personally, I'd rather be lower in weight and feeling confident about myself than self-medicating with food and gaining weight and feeling worse.

I had purchased a bunch of clothes for the Summer at my new weight, and they are now a little snug, making me feel like my summer weight is my winter weight and I missed the shedding of Spring. Know what I mean?

July 21, 2021

Flip The Switch!!!!

A couple of days ago, there was a switch in the way I saw you. I always saw you in a dimly lit room, on your Throne, and you were blurry. I came to you as a little kid and sat on your lap. That's how I always saw you for some reason.

Someone asked, when we think of You, how do we see You, and that was my picture of You. Just the other night, I closed my eyes, and I saw you in a different way. We were walking on a bright and beautiful beach, and we were both dressed in white, walking side-by-side. You were my friend. You loved me. You were listening to me, and you were counseling me, and loving me through your counsel. So grateful to see You in the light and not in a dark space. I think that somewhere, I turned a page, and that is going to change things in life. I love you God!!!

This means something huge, and I cannot wait to see how it unfolds and becomes more of a reality in my life, a new thing that is going to continue to have more meaning.

What am I grateful for? Making my own schedule. Dealing with people I want and not dealing with people who are energy squelchers. Having options and having life on my terms. I need your wisdom to work this right for me. A special way just for me that is comfortable, a comfortable start to get the fire going, and then go from there. I need inertia.

I'd like more and new branches added to my business tree. People who will take advantage of the opportunity and want to grow their own opportunity trees.

I'm grateful to be able to walk and talk with You on this journey, to figure this out. Of course, I did nothing for the business today. Tomorrow is a new day, and I will have more time alone with myself and with You. I can regroup, rethink, and reach out. I am planting my prayer seed in the ground for the desires of my heart.

August 8, 2021

Meeting my friends… a God thing. Ever get a little voice in your head that tells you to go somewhere, to turn somewhere, and you're not sure why, but when you do, you see the surprise that you were supposed to see?

That's how these connections turn out to be so blessed. Yesterday I woke up feeling that the

Lord was going to specially order my steps for the day. I worked out and got ready, had breakfast, and felt led to take some stuff with me to see what needed to be done, be ready for anything, and not go back home.

So, I sat in one of my favorite comfy places, did some scriptural reading to lift my spirits and be closer to the Lord, and get some encouragement as well. While I sat there, I received a text message from a friend I hadn't seen in a while who wanted to meet for coffee. That put me close to a client, so I stopped by to see how she was doing and if there was anything she needed.

I had a great time with a friend who I had not seen in almost two years. We were both in places that were growing periods. Coming together after all this time was so wonderful as we shared our journeys of God's goodness in our lives and what our healing journeys had consisted of.

As we hugged and went our separate ways, planning to meet again, it was such a wonderful feeling of a full 360 to see where our lives are now in comparison to where they were when we first met.

Driving away, I came to a light. I felt led to go to a certain store. It's a little out of the way, and it's a bit of a specialty store, so I don't go often. The pull was strong to go, so I got into the turn lane. Once I was in the lane, I noticed my phone light up. It was another one of my friends letting me know that she was at the store and was asking if I needed anything. I texted back, "one sec," and there she was as I pulled into the parking lot of the store. What a blessed little reunion, as we had been trying to get together for a couple of weeks and kept having to postpone.

I would say that was God, especially ordering my steps that day. It was awesome! Not just one, but several God-winks in one day!

Being in that store was a challenge. I don't go often because for me, it's more of a snack store than it is a staple food store. So, I ended up spending more than I thought on things I really didn't need just because they looked interesting and I wanted to taste them. Because after all, it's still "The Summer of Me!"

So today, I decided to have some of those foods, and it's my choice. Thoughts have been coming to me, and I'm working through my body issues. I'm the one who wants to lose the weight. No one is pressuring me to do it. No one wants me to be skinnier. It's me who feels more comfortable at a lower weight.

I see pictures of myself at lower weights, and I like what I see. I like the way I look, and I remember the way I felt when I was there, and it was a good thing. I was comfortable in my own skin. I was also able to just look in the closet and wear what I wanted. I was choosing that outfit because it looked good, as opposed to wearing something that's going to help me look good because I was trying to hide parts of my body.

I'm having a new peace in my life and I like it. I'm not making the best of choices for myself today, but I'm feeling OK mentally. This is a life journey, not a race to reach the finish line of this weight loss journey, so I can live. It's not a be-all, end-all. It's my way of life. Getting to a more comfortable weight is a short journey. It won't and shouldn't take a lifetime to get there, but maintenance and eating healthier is that lifetime journey.

I'm giving myself mercy and grace. I'm not disgusting, ugly, or horrible-looking as the enemy tries to make me think I am. This warped sense of well-being is not of God.

Tomorrow I will reach for the habit that I had been working on when I first started this journey, and there was something that came up, like an event. That is, eat on the day of the event and the next day, get right back on track without looking back and feeling sorry for myself.

I'm going to get up, do my morning routine of self-care by working out, showering, and taking care of myself without giving my mind the opportunity to "wallow" or let my flesh dwell on what I did the day before. I'm just going to continue to look forward and not look back, to allow that decision to have some treats to make me come undone. That strength will help me with my journey. Giving myself mercy occasionally, not letting the scale affect me in a negative way. That feels empowering.

August 8, 2021

Non-scale victories
Honeymoon phase with weight loss
Self-inventory

What can you do better so that you can make sure you're doing your best?

The "stuff" that caused you to get to 200 pounds does not disappear with the weight loss.

The number on the scale is a reflection of what's been going on in life, so you can't be mad at the number.

Life-long follow-up.

It takes a year for the metabolic set point to take place in the body to reset your new set point.

It shouldn't be this hard to be a person.

I can't go to my happy place with food anymore.

Your past is your past, and if you continue to dwell there, you will not be able to fully and successfully continue towards the abundant future that awaits you.

I'm not going to let what I see in my reflection get me down and discourage me.

Extended obedience in the same direction.

There is so much to be said about the family unit and what happens to a child when that unit is broken.

Illusion and reality finally came together today, and, like I suspected, illusion didn't stand a chance.

If you don't adjust your mindset, this will not work.

Analyze your emotions rather than feel them, so you will not be beholden to them.

Taking a leap of faith into the unknown seems impossible unless you're willing to replace fear with hope.

Sometimes, the only apology you can give for how you've lived your life is to change it completely.

Food is how we celebrate; it's how we have a good time. It's happiness to many people.

August 14, 2021

Truth provides guidelines, blueprints, pathways, structures, and boundaries in our lives so we won't live any old kind of way.

August 15, 2021

Choices. We all have them. Every minute of every day, we have a choice. A choice to do the right thing, to help someone to stay on the right path, to do good or do evil, to be yourself or to be someone else.

Even in the middle of a bag of chips, you can stop and get on the right track. You have a choice to put it down right now and get on the path at this moment, or you can choose to keep going and start when the chips have all been eaten.

My little summer fling is almost over. I have enjoyed it very much, and I am grateful for the time I've had. School starts tomorrow, and I'm starting back on my macro. I am determined to finish this race I started and be on my way to maintenance forever.

Reaching the finish line would be such a thrill and a huge milestone, plus a big check off my life goal list. Maintenance would be a little plus on that list.

A faith-based approach to weight loss… remember when you asked God to help you at 205? He told you to cut portions and eat half of what you were eating.

Yesterday, I was reading a scripture that is a source of hope for me, of God's goodness and restoration. The widow woman with the oil… 2 Kings 4. What is in your house, in you, that can be poured out for others? What's in your vessel that can be poured out for and to others? We have all had an experience or experiences that *we can share with others. When we go through things, they're not just for us. The wisdom gained can benefit others. The wisdom and experience can help them on their journey to avoid potholes they've already seen and hit.*

There are debts and deficits in your body... life has broken you, there is not enough in you. Then you go through something, and that something produces something precious, a beautiful oil. That oil can be poured out and distributed to others. In doing so, this will not only help you, but help others as well.

Pouring out that oil benefits you because sharing benefits others, and helping others always makes us feel good. Wisdom can be gained by what we've gone through, and, if possible, the wisdom of others is always a better choice than hurtfully gaining that wisdom ourselves. That's not to say that we're not going to go through anything, but if you're on the precipice of something and someone else has already gone through it, why not draw on their wisdom for a less hurtful, damaging, and painful experience? Let that oil pour out into as many vessels as you can to bring comfort, peace, joy, and purpose to those who cross your path or your reach.

When I first started my journey, I was numb, but in being numb, I just carried forth to the next best step. I followed the course set before me and just continued on my path. I trusted God to help me on this journey. He graciously provided the hope that I needed to move forward and to trust what the professionals had put before me. The way things were lining up, it was as if God Himself had put this plan together just for me.

For the longest time, this was like a secret. I was able to keep it to myself and not share much. Few people knew what was going on and I liked it that way. Going through breast cancer was such a personal thing that I preferred to keep to myself.

About a year later, I met with a friend, and I shared the experience with her. I was still in my incognito mode and shy about sharing publicly what had happened privately. Not long after our visit, she asked if she could have the name of my doctor, as she had shared my experience with someone who had gone through something similar, yet her journey was not as successful.

I was furious at first. I had privately shared what had happened with her, and here she was telling someone else about it. I put down my phone, and I just went back to cooking dinner. I gently felt the Holy Spirit tap me on the shoulder, clearing His throat and saying gently... "you didn't just go through this for yourself, this is an experience and a pathway to be shared with others." I couldn't believe what I was hearing. Was the very God who I trusted and hid myself in asking me to out myself? UGH! Instead of retaliating and leaving a nasty message, I sent the name of the doctor.

I realized that it was now time to come out of the closet, come out of hiding, come out of the room where I was, and start blessing others with my journey. As people came into my path, I was to share, with discernment, to be a source of help for their pain, and comfort them with peace.

There was an oil inside of me that I had to pour into other vessels to bring them to a place of hope, peace, and ultimate victory.

I'm not the only one who has this oil. We all have it. We all have some experience that we can share with others. It's meant to help others too. With God, nothing we experience is ever wasted.

I am a firm believer that, as the Word says, God is the giver of every good and perfect gift. So, to me, if it's not good, and it's not perfect, and it doesn't have His expected end, it didn't come from Him. So, just like the three fish and five loaves that yielded twelve baskets of leftovers, He doesn't waste anything from our experiences. Not only does He not want us to waste, He also wants us to share them.

Being a closet person, an introvert that is, the last thing this little person wants to do is to share what's happened to her. I didn't want to be looked at as "the girl with cancer". I didn't want special treatment or for people to look at me like "awwww, you poor thing" or "bless your little heart." So, I kept things to myself.

I knew there was a time and place for the secrecy, that there was a window for it and God allowed it, but now it was time to say things when needed. I had to keep my peace, and if and when the opportunity presented itself, then I would share whatever needed to be shared to help their experience be easier and more bearable.

So, what experiences in your life are the oil that will be the balm to help ease the pain of the people in your path? What can you do to help others? Is your vibration turned up so that you can recognize the opportunity that's being set before you? Be a little more alert to the life that's going on around you and more aware of what others are going through so that you can help.

Experiences are not meant for us to turn into ourselves, hide, and never come back out, holding the pain close to our hearts, and letting it ferment. Let it be like oil that flows and heals, bringing richness to the lives of others. You have a worthy story and I bet it's a really good one. It doesn't have to be a book or something big, it can just be to share your experience with your neighbor.

Jesus was the original oil "The Balm," and we are an extension of Him, so let's be that to others, an extension of Him and a balm to them.

August 19, 2021

I'm numb. I slept for 10 hours last night. I have been in pain for a few days. Some moments are excruciating. Others just dull pain. I haven't worked out in two days because I want to rest my body to see if it helps with the pain.

I'm getting ready to embark on another journey of intensity toward my goal of weight loss to get to my desired weight. My Summer of fun is turning into Fall, and it's time to get ready for the leaves to fall. The leaves being my weight. My tree has been growing lots of leaves and is now full and it's time to shed some of this weight and let some of these leaves fall off this tree.

I'm tired and getting ready to start a new schedule. I have been eating things that I've started to like, and I don't want to stop. I know that the treats aren't great for me, but I really don't care. I just want to have fun for now.

Birthdays are coming up, and one last hoorah will be alright. Then it's back to it until I'm done. As much as I can, I'm going to stick to it.

August 23, 2021

Summer is over, and the detour has ended. It's time to get back on the main road and start traveling towards the original destination. I'm going to keep my head down and do whatever is needed to get this done quickly. I may do a sequence of different things. I've tried to keep the fires going, and then when I'm within 5 pounds, I am going to do the metabolism boost to recharge and reset to build muscle.

Today was supposed to be the start date, but we're putting it off until tomorrow. The first meal was what it was, but all is well... the rest of the day can be salvaged.

I'm still debating the lemon, vinegar, and cayenne pepper cleanse for a few days, then 2 weeks of my power plan, and continuing that intermittently with 17-day or belly fat tea cleanse until I'm close to finishing. The rest, a combination of all my plans so I don't get bored.

I went from being 15 pounds from my goal weight to being 35 pounds from my goal weight. Sweet Jesus! The Summer of Me really had an effect, but it was a choice, and now I'm living with the consequences of that choice. I'm hoping that the first 10 is easy since most of the eating has been done in the past few days due to the birthday celebrations.

I am praying that this journey helps someone. This is crazy if you look at it with physical eyes. I remember a time when I was struggling to get below the 150's, where every meal counted because that one could put you 1-3 pounds over, which would undo a week's worth of work. Now, here I am, way over that and starting not from scratch, but from a place that is much further away than what was intended.

So, a new journey begins, and I'm looking forward to getting the sugar out of my system in order to be clearer, with greater perspective and more energy.

I feel so full right now. I felt the same way last night. Not in the "I just ate too much way," but in the "I'm done with this thing way. I'm just done partying and polluting myself. I've taken this as far as I wanted to go and we're done."

September 26, 2021

Have weekly checkups with yourself like going to the doctor until you get better so you can assess your progress and where you need tweaking.

Schedule regular visits with yourself... like you have coffee with a friend to catch up, have coffee with yourself to strategize what you're going to do, put a plan in place, and then schedule regular visits to see how you're doing and keep up with your progress. Doing this on a regular basis will keep you accountable to yourself and your plan. It will also help in nipping things in the bud so that you're moving in a positive direction. You'll also be able to measure your progress, and as you move along, you will see what tweaks need to be made in the event there are any lags in your progress. You can check in on those lags, see why you're lagging, and nip it before it gets bigger. Quality and quantity control with yourself.

This kind of checking in will help you with any pitfalls or any delays in your progress, and will help you to stay on track. If too much time goes by without proper assessment, then things pile up, and it's a bit more of a challenge to get back on your course.

Some good questions to ask ourselves daily are... How was my day? Did I laugh a little and have a good time? How did I feel about the day overall? What are my take-aways from this day's experiences? What would you keep? What would you change or do differently?

December 29, 2023

What are you waiting for?
Are you in "earnest" about being whole?

I'm in the middle of a study on John, and I was pondering the parable of the man at the pool of Bethesda who had been waiting 38 years for his healing.

John didn't give much background on him, only that he suffered from a long, deep-seated, lingering disorder. John also writes that Jesus knew what was troubling him and asked him one simple question: "Do you want to be made whole?"

There have been many times in my life where I've felt the Lord ask me this same question, and as I'm wrapping up this year and the new one is approaching, I'm hearing it again.

The man's response was a dissertation of the circumstances. How often do we do that? Tell God "the whole" story as if Jesus doesn't know.

His simple question to us is, "Do you want to be made whole?" Basically asking, do you want to start thriving instead of just surviving?

He wants us to answer that question because our answer will determine what happens next. A "no" response will allow it to linger. A "yes" will follow with instructions from the Holy Spirit, who will guide us through.

Jesus wants us to be whole, not just healed, but whole. In other gospels, Jesus asks, "What do you want me to do for you?"

As we begin this New Year, here are two questions for us: what do we want Him to do for us, and do we want Him to make us whole?

He can and will give us the desires of our hearts if we just turn to Him, leave our excuses behind, and continue to walk in the direction that He has mapped out for us.

Trust Him to meet you at your first step and carry you through. He will never leave you or forsake you, and is willing to help you THRIVE.

Today I was reminded of some passages in the Bible... there were several scriptures about people waiting. People who were hoping for some type of help and healing, whether it was physical or financial. At times, the question was... WHAT DO YOU WANT ME TO DO FOR YOU???

"Do you want to be made whole?" That was the question Jesus asked the man at the pool of Bethesda who had waited for 38 years for someone to stir the waters for him so that he could receive his healing.

He "suffered with a deep-seated and lingering disorder." When Jesus noticed him lying there [helpless], knowing that he had already been a long time in that condition, He said to him, Do you want to become well? [Are you really in earnest about getting well?] AMPC John 5:5-6

We're not sure what was wrong with him specifically, other than that he couldn't walk. There was no background, just that he had been there waiting for 38 years on a mat. He was making excuses as to why he hadn't gotten his healing yet. Jesus already knew his story, and his only question was. "Do you want to be made whole?"

Jesus wants to know what we want and isn't necessarily concerned with our recounting every hurt and wrong, because He already knows it all, and maybe recounting it may hurt us and keep us from getting the healing that we need.

He knows what we've gone through because He has walked it with us, and He wants to offer us healing and comfort. He wants to heal us and set us on the path of abundant life.

The question is... do you want to be made whole? Do you want to live abundantly, to have the life that's in your heart? The blessings He died to give you? Do you want to rehearse your hurt to make sure God knows, or do you just want the blessing, the cookie that God is offering you from His beautiful jar, partake of that snack, and just be healed?

CHAPTER 18

Tips On How To Get In The Zone

There are steps we can take to help us get into this zone. Motion helps us to get there. It usually happens once we act on a healthy thought or goal we've been thinking about. Moving in the direction of our goals and dreams gives us strength. As we rack up the littlest of wins, we will continue to be fueled by them.

Some think that you must feel it first, and then the rest will come. For me, and some I've known and coached, the opposite is true. We've waited so long for that "feeling" that never comes, so we sit still, afraid, not moving or growing. I'm not saying to do things haphazardly or without enlisting the help of the Holy Spirit through prayer. I'm asking you to move when necessary and not wait for the goosebumps, the "feel goods," to come to you before you do something. Jesus, who I look up to and model my life after, went to the cross because that was God's will. He knew He had to go. He waited until His hour, and then He prepared Himself and did what was necessary. There were no feel goods there. He knew what He had to do and He went and did.

We must have conviction in our hearts that this is the path we're supposed to walk, and whether we feel it or not, we're moving forward because this belongs to us. A word from experience, not every light on the road of life is going to be green. There will be stops, pauses, and go's on our life journey. If you're waiting for all greens, you will never move off your street, let alone reach your destination.

Frame the Day - start well to end well, and do what's required in between. Make time to get up and go to sleep in a way that will be a blessing to your day and your night. Waking up on the wrong side of the bed can make for a tough day. So can going to bed unsettled with stuff on your mind. Going late and feeling frazzled does not make for a good night's sleep. We must ease into our nights the same way we ease into our days.

I have a morning and evening routine that I follow. No matter what's going on, I make sure that I'm able to follow them as consistently as I can. Are there days when things don't go the way I planned? Sure. However, for the most part, I do my best to stick to those routines and have learned to pivot to make the best of each day by fitting them in.

Shake off the gunk that makes you feel guilty when things don't go the way you planned. At least you have a plan and system in place, even if it doesn't go 100% your way every day. When your mind and body know what's coming, they are more at ease. Systems help us organize our lives and ourselves, bringing harmony to our bodies. Finding our rhythm in the day helps things go more smoothly, which increases the peace in our lives.

Speaking of rhythm, let's face the music - when something unpleasant happens, you're faced with adversity or uncertainty, it's best to sit back, assess the situation, and then face it. Find the best solution to the situation with the knowledge you have, and if you're stumped, get help so you can keep moving.

I sit back, close my eyes, keep quiet, and mentally pray first. I bring it to God before I mouth off, for the most part. Throwing spaghetti at the wall to see what sticks doesn't usually work for me. However, bringing it before God, assessing it, and waiting for an answer has helped me tremendously and has saved me from potentially tumultuous situations as well. I found that coming in guns blazing, unless the situation granted that type of entrance, did not help.

Hiding and not facing it doesn't help either. For months, I just let myself go. I let myself do what I wanted without much regard for the consequences that I was going to have to face. I was letting myself just go off the rails, jump the fence, and run wild. That's OK once in a while, but at some point, you have to come home and face life head-on and do what's necessary to deal with what's happening. Avoiding something doesn't make it go away, nor does it make things better. Doing what's right at the moment and facing it like an adult are the best things we can do for ourselves and those around us.

Of course, if you're not sure what to do, keep praying, seek wise counsel, and then move on that wise counsel. I don't mean call ten of your friends and family members and then come up with the best common denominator solution. Your life shouldn't be like a democracy. God should get the final vote. For me, and many others I've walked with and coached, this has been the best approach.

Budget your body, energy, and food like you budget your checkbook. Balance is something that can happen in every area of life. You can have all the plates up in the air without them falling on your head. If each one is given the attention it deserves, they will serve you well and stay up. Your body has a budget just like everything else. Get familiar with what it's telling you. If you're in the black, keep going. If you're heading towards the red, then you need to stop before you're overdrawn. We must make deposits more frequently than we make withdrawals to keep staying in a healthy state of mind and body.

Running yourself ragged by burning the candle at both ends, unless you're up against a deadline and it's a necessary thing that needs to be done with an end in sight, doesn't help anyone finish well, or at times, finish at all, for that matter. Pacing ourselves helps us be balanced and even-keeled.

Our mindset matters. I'm sure you've heard this a million times... what you think about, you bring about. The way you see and think of yourself deep in your heart is what will materialize in your life. Whether you speak it or not, the way you see it with your inner eye and heart is what eventually comes to pass. That is the first place we start, in our minds, and then, if we continue down that path with that thought, positive or negative, that is what manifests in our lives.

Where your thoughts go, your mouth follows, and then your body and life eventually turn in that direction. So, unless you like what you see and you want to continue on that path, change your thoughts. Replace those negative pictures and words with positive ones. Pictures of wholeness, healing, and victory.

When you get a thought about something to eat, and a certain food pops up in your brain, what do you do with that thought? Do you follow it instead of dismissing it? Do you continue with the thought and let it take you down a rabbit hole?

What worked for you in the past? Can you put it together and make a soup, using a blend of what you have learned, what you are comfortable with that is easy to follow until your brain and body have defogged and you can think clearly? Any movement in the proper direction is better than no progress at all.

CHAPTER 19

Some Final Thoughts...

What needs to happen for you to say "this has been the best year of my life?"

Don't know where to start? Project forward, start with the final scene, decide how you want it to end, and then work backwards to the start. It is called reverse engineering your goal or outcome. You see the final product, then break down all the steps of how to get there. You can be as specific and meticulous as you like.

God wants all of us to be whole. Wholeness is when there is no longer a sign of anything that you have gone through., restoration, like it never happened. Like the Old Testament story of the leper or the woman with the issue of blood, that is the difference between healing and wholeness.

Coming to a place where you cannot even remember how bad it was, because it's a faint and blurry memory of the past. It's like you have put in all the work and are doing it day by day, forming new habits, renewing your mind to the possibility of "I can" instead of "I can't." Until one day, you wake up, and you are right in the middle of your dream. You have to pinch yourself because you have waited for this reality forever.

What you repeatedly hear, you eventually believe. Your mind believes your own voice more than anyone else's. Speak to yourself. Speak truth, speak your goals, speak how you want this year to end.

Do not look back, like Lot's wife, who was urged to leave a city that was about to be destroyed. Run forward toward what God has for you. She chose to look back and was turned into a pillar of salt. I think there is a great analogy here. She became stagnant and immobile to the point of death. You can be destroyed by looking back in ways that are more nostalgic towards the past than the future God has for you. Look ahead.

Everything God has for you is ahead of you, not behind you. Stop talking about your past, replaying it in your mind, and rehearsing the stories. Stop reminding God about it and asking Him to forgive you for it. He forgave you the first time you asked.

Give your past a burial!

A person with no vision will focus on the familiar and return to their past instead of intentionally forging their future in hopes of fostering change and victory. They are afraid of the unknown so they stay in their comfort zone, clinging to what they know instead of taking a moment to be brave and do something different, sowing towards their dream future. Each moment of small, intentional bravery creates that compound effect, strengthening us to consistently do BIG things. Like a child on a tricycle who has just had the training wheels taken off, the further we go, the more confident we become until we are riding without thinking about pedaling or falling.

If you do not have a vision for your life, you will remain stagnant. If you do not have a vision for your body, you will go back to your prior weight; if you do not have a vision for your money, you will go back into debt. You cannot have a million-dollar dream with minimum wage habits.

A tracked number creates success. Failure to track these areas leads to being stuck and drifting. Before you go too far out to sea, get the help you need to understand where you are, and where you would like to be. Then, create a specific plan to live you best and most abundant life.

CHAPTER 20

Peace in Restoration

"Instead of your shame you shall have double honor,
And instead of confusion they shall rejoice in their portion.
Therefore in their land they shall possess double;
Everlasting joy shall be theirs."
Isaiah 61:7 (NKJV)

One of the first things I think of when I hear the word restoration is wiping the slate clean. I think of do-overs where it looks like the very thing that happened never happened. Everything is back to its original state, as if you've gone back in time and erased it from ever taking place.

The ultimate act of restoration took place on the cross when Jesus re-established our broken relationship with the Father. We were redeemed from the sin in the Garden through Him and restored to that initial moment of personal fellowship with God and our intimate relationship with Him. All our sins were wiped clean, and we can now go boldly to the Throne of God for any and every thing.

God's restoration is greater than we can ask or think because when God restores, not only does it seem like He's set the clock back, He smooths all things out and provides a valuable lesson for us that leaves a beautiful, indelible mark, like a gentle, loving kiss on our cheek.

I have been the recipient of His restoration many times in my life. Because of my upbringing, the looking glass of others and their religious beliefs, I was led to believe in a God that was different from what the Word portrays Him to be.

This caused me to have distorted and warped thought patterns, rooted in immense guilt, that provoked me to go my own way many times in life. Like the Apostle Peter, I had many short bursts of faith. My proclamations were strong one minute, then when faced with struggles or low moments, I turned to my flesh.

The Lord used people, music, and His Word to gently restore my relationship with Him each time I strayed. I am so grateful for the sacrifice of Jesus as this helped me to realize that I am worthy to be restored because of Him.

My most vivid experience with this precious restoration was when I first heard about the veil that was torn in the temple when Jesus exhaled His last breath. Seeing that in the Word showed me that there was no longer anything keeping me from going directly to the Father.

I didn't have to say "x" amount and "types" of prayers to be exonerated and restored to Him. I no longer had to carry the guilt and shame of what my sin had caused because it was taken in by Jesus, exhaled from His breath on the cross, and evaporated into the air. His blood covered every little thing I did, and when He said it was finished, it was. There's nothing else for us to do other than go to Him and ask His forgiveness. He is faithful to forgive us.

I used to keep away from God because of the religious belief that I was unworthy to go to Him when I sinned. I was dirty, and He was Holy, so I had to go through someone else to get free, and even then, there was still a debt owed, and expedition for these sins after death. Jesus made it possible for me to go directly to the Father. I didn't need a mediator because Jesus was that Man. Jesus pulled back that curtain. The veil has been removed, and now I can go directly to God. He sees me through the blood of Jesus, all is forgiven, and I am restored every single time.

One day, in Psalm 103, I saw a list of benefits for the soul that trusts and believes in Him. That His mercies are great towards us, and He has separated us from our sins, as far as the east is from the west. I'm familiar with east and west, but think about it, if you're on the east side of the world and you start heading west, you will continue to go east and never really reach west, you never catch up to it, that is how far He has put our sins away from us. Once He has forgiven them, we never catch up to them again. Selah.

My salvation and sense of redemption did not come easily. I remember sitting in an empty church one day, staring at a crucifix hanging from the ceiling. It was a beautiful, rustic church on top of a hill, and it was a grey and windy day. No one was there but me and God. The voices of those in my life were so heavy on my heart and in my mind that I did not know where to turn, so I came here to find refuge.

I remember sitting there, staring up at the cross, listening to the whistling of the wind through the church as I cried out to God for the truth. I just wanted the truth. I wanted what God wanted, and to stop the confusion of what others were saying a relationship with Him should be. I looked at the crucifix, and I cried in a loud voice spiritually and physically. The only words I could muster were that I wanted Him, His truth, just The Truth!

Those words, asking for The Truth, soon melted away a veil within my heart. I could feel the power of the Lord overtake the church and permeate my body, my heart, and my mind. The experience is something I will never forget. It was as if the Lord personally came to show me that Jesus was the truth, that all I needed was Him, and that all was well.

The scornful, judgmental voices and the accusatory pointing fingers in my mind were now gone. The torment, shame, and deep oppression my sin had caused were gone. The Holy Spirit took over, and there was new life within me. The burdens of the past were no longer on my back and infused in my being.

I had never felt that type of restorative peace before. The Scripture of becoming a new creature rang true for the first time in my life as if new blood was now flowing through my veins. Like a dry-erase board, all the scribbles were wiped away, and it was once again white and clean, as if nothing had ever been written against me. I felt one with God, Jesus, and the Holy Spirit. The darkness of my sins and my past was replaced with the light of the Father's fellowship and immense love.

It was difficult to accept this love. I did not understand it. I was not used to it, and I had not seen it before. The love I was used to was clouded by others' pain and life experiences projected onto me. So, this deep and pure love that I was experiencing from God was almost unbelievable.

The Lord is a Master at saving and sparing. He continually saves us and spares us from tragedies, even though we may not think it at the time. Looking back, I can see how He was always there for me and was pouring blessings into my life right in the middle of huge and disturbing messes. Like my sweet Jesus, saying, "I'm sorry your cake fell to the floor. Here, have a cookie; it tastes better, you'll see." 😄

My favorite stories of restoration in the Bible are of the 10 lepers in Luke 17, Jairus's daughter and the woman with the issue of blood in Mark 5, and of course, the ultimate restoration, Jesus's resurrection. These instances stand out to me most because of the way they happened and how they relate to my life.

The story of the leper taught me that Jesus restores what is eaten away, and He gives us extra for our gratefulness. He put everything back for that leper. The scripture does not get specific, but what if his fingers, face, nose, and who knows what else were missing as a result of the leprosy, and they all grew back as he walked away? Not only would he have the smooth skin of a baby, but he was also made whole because he went back and expressed his gratitude. There is a difference between healing and wholeness. Healing takes care of what's ailing you, but wholeness restores everything in your life and body back to its original form and then some!

There were 10 lepers in that accounting of healing. Only one of the 10 men came back to thank Jesus. Because of this one leper's gratefulness, he was the only one who was made whole.

Jesus even said, "Were there not ten cleansed? But where *are* the nine?" (Luke 17:17 NKJV) To top it off, the one that came back was a "stranger," a "foreigner," "a Samaritan!" (v.18) He was not a Jew who had grown up with the Scripture promises and in anticipation of a Messiah. He was an outsider with different ways of worship, not of the lineage of Jesus and the chosen people.

He said to him, "Arise, go your way. Your faith has made you well." (Luke 17:19 NKJV)

As the man went, he saw his healing, and he cried out in a loud voice and glorified God. Then, he ran toward Him, fell at His feet, and thanked Him for his healing. There on the ground, he worshiped the MAN God who had healed him. Jesus, of the line of David, the promised Messiah, took the time to heal a leprous Samaritan. This man had two strikes against him. He was a leper and a Samaritan. Yet Jesus reached out to him, willingly accepted him, and healed him.

Think of what this healing did for this man. He was completely ostracized from society because of this disease. The lepers were standing on the sidelines because they could not be close to people. They were considered unclean, outcasts, and social rejects. The healing and wholeness that Jesus provided restored all those areas of his life. He could now go back to his family, his work, and his life before this disease made him a recluse. As an added bonus, he has this awesome experience of meeting the living God to take with him.

Then we have the story of Jairus and the woman with the issue of blood. These stories, in particular, have great meaning to me. I have come to realize that, in a sense, I am both Jairus and the woman with the issue of blood. When I read this passage in Scripture, it's like a movie reel starts to play in my head.

I am walking with Jesus and explaining my situation. There are people everywhere, and I'm taking a big risk being out here with Him. However, I cannot deny the proof in the Torah of the promise of Him to us. In the middle of our deep conversation, He stops in His tracks and asks who touched Him. He felt the touch of faith drawing on His power, and He wanted to know who touched Him with that intensity. She reveals herself. Wait, I know her. She used to come to our synagogue until she was diagnosed with bleeding and was forced out of community. Stories of her imply that she lost practically everything because of this bleeding, and now, Jesus, through her faith, has healed her.

As Jesus is listening to her story, I look over, and I see them coming. Their faces do not look good at all, and they bring the news I was dreading. Just as the last words leave their lips, Jesus whirls around as if He can hear the thoughts in my mind and the fear in my heart, His cloak swaying about Him as He turns, His mouth produces a thunderous yet peaceful voice declaring to me, "Fear not, believe only."

He walks me back to my home, passes by the mourners, and heads straight for my daughter's room. Shutting everyone out besides me, my wife, and His inner circle of Peter, James, and John, He takes her hand and commands her to rise from her sleep. His words and touch, like electricity through her body, jolt her back to life. She opens her eyes, arises, and walks over to hug me. All the hopes and dreams of a father for his daughter come rushing back to me. Jesus has restored all our lives.

I have been Jairus. I have been face-to-face with impossible situations that felt as bad as death at the door, because life as I knew it had died. For a good portion of my life and in different instances, I was also that woman with the issue of blood. I was bleeding in so many areas of my life that it seemed like there wasn't enough gauze to plug up the holes to make it stop. No one could give me the triage I needed but Jesus.

There was physical, emotional, and financial bleeding due to a series of incapacities. The bleeding was also spiritual, causing my faith to be like faulty wiring in an old house, flickering on and off, or dim at best. These very experiences had me on the sidelines of life and deep, meaningful fellowship with God.

Only Jesus could redeem the life I had lost and create a new and worthwhile one for me. This bleeding drained every good thing life had to offer, and the eternity that awaited me. I smelled. I was weak, broke, and alone. I didn't believe God loved me because I was so ill, and that my sins were the cause of it.

I did not fully understand that I could call out to Him and He would rush to me and hug me to Him in a flash. I did not know how to turn to Him, how to call on Him, His Word, or use my authority. I did not even know I had authority and that He had relinquished it to me on the cross. He now lives within me, and that puts me on a spiritual plane that exists only when we proclaim our fellowship with Him. Because of Jesus, I have special power to draw closer to God.

Jairus, the woman, and the leper all had special circumstances and, in one way or another, should not have been going to Jesus. Jairus was a religious leader, and it was frowned upon by the other Jewish leaders to believe in and be around Jesus. In fact, they carried such hatred toward Him that they plotted to kill Him. Our little woman and the leper had been ostracized and became social outcasts because of their physical conditions. Lest we forget, they were both considered to be of lower class as she was a woman and the leper was a Samaritan. So, we can add the complications of minority and nationality to their list.

Jesus demonstrated that He was no respecter of persons and rewarded their faith by performing miracles, plugging up the holes in their lives, and making them whole again. Raising a beloved daughter from the dead and proving to those who chose to believe that He was the Son of God, and He was performing these miracles.

Jesus did not fault the woman for coming forward despite their Levitical laws. In fact, He commended her for her faith and acknowledged it in front of her entire community. She was now free to live her life, and all was restored to her. The leper was restored physically and socially, as a Samaritan, was accepted by Jesus.

Not only did God restore them on this earth, He also restored them to heaven. His sacrifice tore the veil that was withholding us from an unhindered relationship with God so that we can go straight to His Throne. Our sins and tears have been washed away, and are able to go directly into the Holy of Holies to partake in the Father's fellowship and get the help we need at any time.

Our relationship and right standing with God have been renewed because of Him. We are free to draw closer to God. In my heart, we are in two places, here on this earth and in heavenly places, taking full advantage of our blood-bought privileges.

Growing up, I did not know that this sweetness could exist. My understanding of God was warped. He was not a Father or a friend. Now, this newfound restoration allows me the opportunity to live what some call the high life. I am back in the high life again because of Jesus!

There are several Scriptures that refer to our physical, spiritual, emotional, and financial restoration. Some of my other favorites are… Job, where the Lord restored double what he had lost, in Joel the Lord restored the years that were eaten, in Jeremiah He promises to restore our health, in Isaiah He promises to restore our blessing, our joy, give us a double portion, and take away our shame.

Two of my special favorites are John 10:10 and Proverbs 6:31. We know the thief comes to steal and destroy. However, when he is found, he must give back seven times what was stolen. In essence, I'm too expensive for him to mess with because God has equipped me with His Word and His authority to live an abundant life.

God promises restoration to His church, His people. It is His desire. Like the lepers, Jairus, and the woman with the issue of blood, we can also claim our restoration. With bulldog faith, we can hang on until our miracles come, praising Him for it through our struggles, knowing in our hearts that He is faithful. What He did for others, He will do for us. We can call on Him to get help in our time of need and rise in fellowship with Him here, and eventually rise like Jesus, to heaven in our new, resurrected bodies when we leave this earth. Through belief in Jesus, God promises restoration to us on either side of heaven.

CHAPTER 21

For Such A Time As This

"Do not think in your heart that you will escape in the king's palace any more than all the other Jews. For if you remain completely silent at this time, relief and deliverance will arise for the Jews from another place, but you and your father's house will perish. Yet who knows whether you have come to the kingdom for *such* a time as this?" (Esther 4:13-14 NKJV)

The past few years have been so uncertain for many of us. A shroud has been over people, like netting in a sci-fi movie that is holding them back, keeping them cocooned or immobile with an overwhelming fear of moving forward and making purposeful changes.

For me, the cocoon was meant to protect me and help me grow in my spiritual walk during these years. This growth helped me to better understand and cling to Romans 15:4, "For whatever things were written before were written for our learning, that we through the patience and comfort of the Scriptures might have hope." (NKJV)

This passage was written way before the season of Covid. God knows the beginning and the end. He knows what is going to happen in our future. Because of this passage and many others, I had the hope and strength I needed to break through. I was able to glean and learn from this experience through the hope that can only be found in His Word.

It was now time to break free from that cocoon and become the butterfly that God created me to be. Since the beginning of time, God has wanted an abundant life for us (John 10:10). His desire is for us to be mentally and physically agile, to go about our lives and His Kingdom business.

Self-care during these past few years has gone in two directions. Some have increased their cognizance of taking care of themselves and have extensively explored different ways of doing so. Sadly, others have gone in another direction. They have given up essential care for themselves and thus have spiraled downwards spiritually, mentally, physically, and emotionally.

We may have days, weeks, and seasons where we are rocking our self-care, but then something happens. Our brains and emotions are not prepared for that particular life curveball, and we fall back to our familiar habits of not prioritizing our self-care. We stay up longer than our bodies can handle. We eat more than necessary or make unhealthy food choices because those foods bring us the comfort we desperately need. We revert to our tendency to calm ourselves with things that can hinder or hurt us.

Let's look back to another time in history, 473 B.C. I would like to journey with you to a story in the Bible, the Book of Esther, when life was not going well for the Jewish people. Their disobedience and idolatry as a nation opened a door for them to be taken captive by the Babylonians and Assyrians. In this story, they were about to be annihilated by an enemy in pursuit of political power, who was so full of pride and disdain for them that he became determined that nothing would stand in his way to facilitate their destruction.

The Book of Esther is one of the few books that bears the heroine's name, and God's name is not mentioned once. Esther became queen during this time in Israel's captivity. A testament to the fact that God is always with us and can give us favor and increase, even in the direst of situations.

One of the first protocols prescribed for her as she was transitioning from her captivity to the harem, and potentially to the King's bedroom, was a full year of beauty treatments. These treatments each had their specific purpose. They were designed to disinfect, moisturize, protect the skin, and aid mental and physical elevation.

In this book, Esther was being prepared for a specific mission. In order to fulfill part of that mission, these treatments were necessary. What type of treatments do you need to help better accomplish your purpose in life? What type of self-care can you incorporate and practice that will help propel you in a positive direction and will bless your future and the future of those around you? What habits, practices, and strategies can you put in place to heal you on the inside and the outside, so you match like a carefully crafted and styled outfit?

These treatments and the favor from those attending to her helped Esther in her next chapter of life. She could draw on the favor God had given her to help her when the time came to make a crucial decision. This decision required wisdom and tenacity.

How do we approach God when faced with difficult situations? Esther's example was awe-inspiring. Although she was unsure how she could help at first, her next actions were to seek God through prayer and fasting. This led to the answer she needed. Fasting and prayer elevated her understanding and gave her the direction she needed, ultimately saving her people.

When we are at the top of our game, close to the Spirit, gleaning our peace and guidance from Him, we can more easily help others be on top of their game in life and share examples of the miracles that hope in God can create.

In July of 2020, the Lord gave me the word "Crown" from Psalm 103, a Psalm of David, verse 4, in The Passion Translation, "You've rescued me from hell and saved my life. You've crowned me with love and mercy."

This is one of my favorite Psalms because of the way it starts, asking God to bless our souls and for our souls to bless God and with the reminder for us not to forget all the benefits He provides.

I later heard the Lord expand on that word and say to me that He was going to crown the year. Psalm 65:11 says, "You crown the year with Your goodness, And Your paths drip with abundance." I'm Italian, and the word "Corona" translated to "Crown," and when I saw that, I had an "Oh Wow" moment.

At the time, I had no idea what that Word would mean for me. The world was in upheaval by the middle of March. My surroundings seemed uncertain. Churches, businesses, and schools were closing all around us. But deep within me, I was determined and hopeful that God would somehow make that scripture a reality in my life.

I went into task mode. With the Holy Spirit as my guide, I was going to rock this Covid thing. I went to bed early to help with my circadian rhythm. I got up, worked out, showered, and got into clean jammies. We all remember those multiple sets, right?

I took care of my body, ate well, and put systems in place to get a handle on what I could control because there seemed to be so many things at that time that were beyond our control.

The year culminated in losing track of my precious brother Joey, who lived in Italy. He was nowhere to be found, and his phone kept going to voicemail. I prayed, and the skies opened. Little bits of information started to trickle in. Someone said that he had fallen and was rushed to the hospital. Another said that he coded while in transit, so they air-lifted him to another hospital that could better help him.

After months of trying to track down which hospital he was in, getting bits and pieces of third-hand information on his condition, we finally learned, in a very displeasing way, that he had passed away. It's funny how the enemy takes the hatred that's within people and allows them to use the deliverance of news as a sword to intentionally pierce and wound our hearts.

Because of the strength and peace that had been built up with my consistent time with God throughout the year, I saw it for what it was and did not waver. Like Esther, I knew where that ugly thing was coming from, and I took action in the spirit and proceeded with His guidance in the natural.

Despite the bewilderment and grief I was experiencing, the Lord brought people into my life to help me with my specific desires to remedy the situation in the best way possible from an ocean away. What I could not do with my own hands, the Lord did for me, and He answered the desires of my heart for my brother in ways that only He could.

With all that was happening, and the entanglements of the legal and international red tape, the Blood of Jesus over the situation was more powerful than all those ugly weapons forged against me. Although the situation seemed hopeless, the Lord was working on my behalf.

And with this grief, you guessed it, the scripture, Psalm 65:11, came to my mind. "So, God, how will You crown this year for me?" was my question to Him. I was trying to stand on that specific Word to glean hope in a hopeless situation.

Memories started flooding in. I started remembering that my brother had talked about this day since my Dad's diagnosis of Lewy Body Disease and imminent death in 2016. Joey couldn't picture a life without my Dad, even making the statement that he wasn't going to be living too long after him. He was miserable in his own body, and as I reflected, I realized that in one fell swoop, God answered everybody's prayers. Life was now different, again, with the loss of another key person in my life.

In Isaiah 43:19, the Lord says that He is about to do a new thing. This was definitely a new thing. I think He's consistently bringing us all new things. With that, I think He's been asking us to put our self-care first. For us to start caring for the temples that He specifically envelops us in, so that we can live more fulfilled lives and have a greater impact on the lives of those around us.

It's time to break free from the webbing and intentionally take back our temples. To have our armor ready and get ahead of "IT" (whatever the "IT" is for you) before "IT" gets ahead of us, and not be like frogs, who cannot feel heat in a pot of nicely warm water, thinking we are relaxing in a luxurious bath, only to succumb to our circumstances.

You see, frogs are cold-blooded little creatures. Their body temperatures are the same as their environments. This means that if the water is gradually heated, the frog will slowly adjust to the change in temperature just as it would in nature. Not realizing that the rising heat is a threat, it eventually takes their lives. Because they kept adapting, those consistent adaptations ultimately led to their demise.

It is time to wake up and see what is going on around us, not just from a world-view, but a spiritual view, which is more important. It is time to break free from the shroud and live the life we were intended to live. To come out of our captivity and be free to live, worship, and be at peace. Like Lazarus, Jesus is calling us to come forth, take off the grave clothes, and eat something that will nourish us, give us strength, and keep us alive. (John 11:43-44)

Peace is possible in every situation. Just like you can start your diet right in the middle of eating a bag of potato chips, it is that one decision that gives us the resolve to take that next best step.

In everything we face, like Esther, we can go to The Throne Room and get the help we need for the specific time that it's needed. Our God is an ever-present help in time of danger. (Psalm 46:1)

How did God crown my year? In the midst of these horrific circumstances, He found magnificent ways to answer the desires of my heart. Blessings came into my life that I never thought would come. Situations that seemed hopeless, where I literally felt crushed on every side, were resolved. Peace was given to so many people around me because their fears were washed away. My brother was given the ultimate peace and rest that he had long desired. And that peace overflowed to others in my family, including myself.

Possibilities and opportunities opened up all around me. New ways of thinking, creating agility in my mind to cope with what was happening around me. New ways of caring and loving. A different way of working and being, which was such a tremendous blessing, and I am continuing to this day.

With all this happening, there were instances where I thought that if I heard the word "pivot" one more time, I would scream. However, having the agility of mind to bounce back, watching my mouth in times of uncertainty, speaking God's truth over the situation instead of speaking the fear that comes with that "first look" were instrumental to me in coping and handling each situation that came up.

I learned from the Holy Spirit how to take better care of my temple. What I put in my mouth, what I heard with my ears, what I saw with my eyes, and what I smelled with my nose became crucial. He showed me how to make my surroundings more inviting for the care I needed to heal and sustain my life. I ate healthier foods, used good skin care and body care daily, listened to positive music, diffused and applied soothing oils to promote peace and tranquility, and open up my mind and heart to receive the healing and comfort I needed at that time. (1 Corinthians 6:19)

We have been so busy with our schedules, false priorities, putting out fires around us, that we have forgotten what matters most. In 3 John 2:2, the Word says that God wants our souls to prosper, and He wants us to be healthy. God wished that for us "above all things." So why are we putting our souls and bodies last?

God is interested in the care of our bodies as much as He is interested in the care of our spirits. There are many references in the Word where

He clearly expresses His expectations for both. He shows us how to care for our bodies to stay physically healthy and how to be in the spirit for the necessary peace of our minds.

In the New Testament, Jesus said that He would never leave us or forsake us. (Hebrews 13:5). He would dwell within us through the Holy Spirit. (1 Corinthians 6:19-20) Our Wonderful Counselor who guides us into all truth, showing us things to come. (John 16:13)

Our physical bodies are now dwellings for the Holy One. Therefore, our temples, just like God's temple, require specific attention and tending to. Let's remember that we are holy and our temple and utensils need to remain clean, unobstructed, and ready for service and worship. Taking care of ourselves is a form of worshipping God. We glorify Him by taking care of the bodies He has entrusted to us.

In his letter to the Romans, Paul's instructions regarding our bodies are very clear: Romans 12:1 tells us, "I appeal to you therefore, brethren, and beg of you in view of [all] the mercies of God, to make a decisive dedication of your bodies [presenting all your members and faculties] as a living sacrifice, holy (devoted, consecrated) and well pleasing to God, which is your reasonable (rational, intelligent) service and spiritual worship." (AMPC)

It is time to adopt what I call a "just go pee attitude." You know…you're lying in bed, and you are slowly waking up, but don't want to get out of bed. We all just want five more minutes. I would say to myself, "Just go pee." After that, the next decision was to flush, wash my hands, and one step at a time, I got to my workout station. I had steps in place to make each decision easy. Like preparing my workout clothes, sneakers, music, water, etc. in advance and having everything I needed ready in my workout room, so I could just walk in, without thinking, put on all my gear, and start my workout.

Getting our minds in motion and focusing on our next best steps is crucial to avoid overthinking a situation. It can make life easier and save us time and aggravation. Refusing to go through the mental swirlings of doubt and indecision, putting our bodies into "I can't" mode freezes our minds and limbs. There is something about the words "I can't" that puts us in a state of immobility and fear. It is so important to let go of fear and remember that this spirit is not of the Lord. (2 Timothy 1:7)

Put strategies in place for yourself that will avoid overthinking and make for a frozen, immobile body. What can you do now to help you later? Is it having a playlist of your favorite songs ready to drown out the enemy? Is it making meals in advance and getting rid of unclean/unhealthy foods in your home that could derail you?

Maybe delete those apps that make it easier to get those foods at your fingertips without leaving your home? How about making a deal with yourself that you will take care of your temple no matter what, and practice getting up 10 minutes earlier every day to do just that? Good hygiene, skin care, and body care do not require much of your time. I often find that it takes more time to think about it than it does to actually do it.

How can you make your home, that special space you have been given, your sanctuary? To make it so that when you walk in and close your door, there is peace all around you, and you can be in a mode that will bring life to your mind and body?

Breathing in the peace and comfort of God, His Word, and His methods will give us the answers that we need to move forward in confidence and victory towards the futures He has forged for us. He has all the tools we need, and He is not holding back on us. By clinging to Him, I learned how to listen, and this softened my heart to His ways. Cling to Him and delight yourself in Him. He never disappoints. I would like to leave you with these little reminders that can have a major impact on your mind and spirit.

Ephesians 3:20, "Now to Him who is able to do exceedingly abundantly above all that we ask or think, according to the power that works in us, to Him be glory in the church by Christ Jesus to all generations, forever and ever. Amen."

2 Corinthians 9:8, which I made as a positive affirmation for myself during this crucial time, "Great grace abounds towards me, so that I, having all sufficiency in all things, requiring no

aid from anyone, am able to give to every good and perfect work."

James 4:8, "Draw near to God and He will draw near to you. Cleanse your hands, you sinners; and purify your hearts, you double-minded."

Psalm 37:4, "Delight yourself also in the Lord, and He shall give you the desires of your heart."

Prayer of faith

Lord Jesus, come into my heart.

I confess that I am a sinner and that I've sinned against Your Holy Name. Forgive me Lord, cleanse me, wash me with your blood.

I confess with my mouth that Jesus Christ is my Lord and my Savior, and I believe in my heart that God the Father raised Jesus from the dead, and I thank you, Father, for putting my name in the Book of Life. Jesus, you are my God, not satan, and I renounce everything that has to do with him.

I forgive from my heart everyone who's ever hurt me, my mom, my dad, everyone, and I ask You, Lord, to forgive me for everyone I've hurt. I receive Your forgiveness and I forgive myself.

I receive salvation and healing in Jesus' Name.

If you have made your first confession of faith or have rededicated your life to Christ Jesus, please reach out to me via the link in my bio, on the platform most convenient for you, so I can pray for you and help you find your next best step in your faith journey.

Ann Marie is a Certified Human Behavioral Specialist, Trainer, Coach, Speaker, Four-time Bestselling Author, Licensed Cosmetologist, Skin Care and Self-Care Enthusiast.

She holds an MA in Business and Ministry and has been empowering people for over 40 years toward reclaiming their confidence, well-being, and purpose by helping them heal and become whole from the "inside out."

She has helped people cultivate an abundance mindset to create lasting, life-transforming habits that allow them to be bold, brave, get off cruise-control, and THRIVE in life.

She believes that when we have an understanding of who we were created to be deep within, it brings courage and strength to accomplish our life's purpose.

Having suffered spinal and traumatic brain injuries, one of her life's quests was to learn how brain function affects our bodies and our lives. Despite the struggles, living without pain was a priority, and she has found ways to engage in life and live abundantly.

Her journey of self-awareness through the study of God's Word fostered her wholeness and well-being. The implementation of this knowledge helped her individually and as an entrepreneur.

Her desire is to share what she has learned with others, help them gain confidence, competence, and wholeness in their minds and bodies to THRIVE, not just survive, in every extension of life.

Ann Marie has spoken on many podcasts and other platforms sharing how to build meaningful and lasting legacies, turning life's challenges, illnesses, and traumas into stepping stones to purpose and resilience to navigate through life.

Connect and get FREE resources in her Skool Community... skool.com/we-thrive-at-life

Find out more and choose your platform on...

https://linktr.ee/wethriveatlife

* 9 7 9 8 9 8 9 4 8 1 1 4 9 *